Through *the* Blue Door

Also in
The BLUE DOOR MEDITATION SERIES:

Through the Blue Door Companion Journal
e-book available only at www.MandorlaAcademy.com/shop

Through *the* Blue Door

A Medium's Guide to Ultra-Sensory
MEDITATION
& Journaling

Heather Oelschlager

Kefi Press

ISBN 978-0-9997082-0-0 (Paperback Edition)

Library of Congress Control Number: 2017918640

Published by Kefi Press
PO Box 174
Hastings, MN 55033

Visit www.MandorlaAcademy.com

Cover art, book design, and illustrations by Heather L. Oelschlager. Original cover photograph by Chance Agrella, FreerangeStock.com.

9 8 7 6 5 4 3 2 1

First paperback edition December 2017
Printed in the United States of America

TABLE of CONTENTS

*Group Variation:
Meditations marked with an asterisk include additional instructions especially for partner or group meditation.

 For Kai

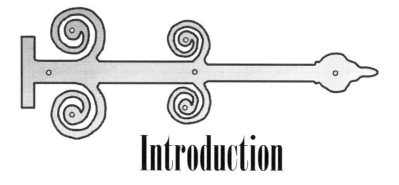

Introduction

THE ROOM IS QUIET. PHONE IS OFF. FAMILY IS OUT FOR THE afternoon. Laundry is in the dryer. The pets fed. No distractions are going to get in the way this time. I am sitting properly on my floor pillow. I am relaxing. Relaxing. My eyes are closed. I am quieting my mind. *Okay, World, I am ready. Bring me the revelations!* Relaxing. Is my mind empty enough? Should I *"Om"*? Does that help? Relaxing. Wait, did I remember to wash my shirt for tomorrow? Yes. Yes, I did. All right, calm my mind. Concentrate and relax. Should something be happening? Am I going to hear something? Maybe I will hear something. This is exciting. It is going to work. I am listening now. Refrigerator running…wall clock ticking. I heard a car drive past. There! Oh, no, that is the cat padding around. Maybe I am going to see something. Darkness. Okay, that is the back of my eyelids, I suppose. Ooh—splotches are moving around! Maybe those are my eyeballs. (Squinting one eye and peeking around the room). No, nothing out there either. (Both eyes closed again). I think I need to stretch out my legs soon. No, I can *do* this. *Concentrate. Empty my mind.* Nope, my foot is starting to fall asleep. Nose itching. The laundry will be done soon. Fidgeting. Restless. *Oh, forget it, maybe tomorrow.*

We have been through it before, attempting to find calm, trying to figure out meditation. So how do we get there, to that promised otherworld of magical insight and imagery? How do we get past all the time spent trying, to the actual *doing*? There is a better way to meditate, a way that will aid in other aspects of your spiritual growth as well, and it is already right in your hands if you are ready to begin.

WHY MEDITATE

As inquisitive human beings, we make an effort to learn and explore. At the heart of it, we want to be better, to know more. Though we might not understand what it is, we want to fulfill our soul's plan, so we strive toward greater awareness. From diverse backgrounds, we are students, readers, writers, teachers, advisors, parents, observers, listeners, visionaries, scholars, scientists, build-ers, artists, farmers, advocates, musicians, entertainers, healers, and guardians. Some have not yet realized their truest capabilities, while others are trying to figure out what to do with them.

Endeavor as we do to understand our life purpose and to accomplish all we can in life, if we are honest, we flounder from time to time. We become stuck; we get frustrated; we make mistakes. We feel alone, we lose hope, and then we somehow find a way to push ourselves again. We find our footing, take a chance, and take the next step on our path. We try, and try again.

Challenges and triumphs fill every human life, but there are ways to ease and overcome the difficulties, as well as to foster the accomplishments, ways not typically taught to us in our childhood. We fail to see that the whole while the Universe is trying to guide us. The Divine, our spirit guides, angels, and most certainly our higher selves (our souls) want us to find our path, because that is the key to us remembering who we are. The truth is that, given the one human absolute of free will, individually we must decide to connect with the Universe; we have to choose to be part of the conversation. To initiate that exchange, one thing is required of us—opening up to our spiritual self. The best news is that it is easier than it sounds, and we already possess everything we need to do it.

Meditation and journaling are two of the most significant resources we can immediately access to tap into our spirituality. They are a means to hold those conversations, to allow ideas, answers, and guidance to come through to us. The meditative experience allows us to explore places we could not travel to see, to connect with our spirit guides, and to use the most accessible tools we have for creating the best in our life. It helps us understand our lives, our purpose, and ourselves. Paired with journaling, it brings greater appreciation and knowledge of our interrelated life experiences. A person who discovers the art of meditation finds a limitless resource for peace, happiness, levity, healing, compassion, and insight.

By learning how to perceive *ultra-sensory* information through the four-step introductory exercises in Part One, and applying those abilities, you will acquire the tools to help you meditate with ease and success. If you have never done meditation before, or if you are someone who has tried to no avail, you will soon find that there is so much more to the process than sitting, waiting for something to happen. On the other hand, perhaps part of your routine already includes time set aside for contemplation, but you are looking to broaden your understanding and options for spiritual exploration. Whatever your previous familiarity, the exercises shared in this book will help you open to greater awareness, find answers to all levels of problems and challenges you face, and access universal guidance.

As you will find in working through the guided meditations, the experiences do not have to be dry, redundant, humorless, or impossible. They need not even be solitary and isolating. Practice all the meditations either individually or as a group activity, with two or more participating. When shared, meditation makes it possible for us to unite with others in spiritual appreciation, acceptance, and harmony. Included within, are meditations that I have taught to my students and clients over a decade working as a medium and teaching spiritual development and non-traditional grief support classes. Fourteen of the meditations include activity aspects to them for more of a workshop dynamic. Some require a little preparation and few extra supplies. You can find these listed together in the Index of Meditations (page 261) under "Activity Meditations."

Throughout the book, you will find that several students and clients generously contributed their own stories to share with you, illustrating how the meditations transpired for them. The intention is not to set direction or expectation for your own adventures, but purely to exemplify variations in purpose, results, tone, and impressions. Consider them shared stories by your remote classmates. Although everyone's experience with meditation is highly personalized and the results are never meant to be the same, sharing the process is decidedly valuable on a level of interconnectedness. It is possible to find this bond through meditating with others or through shared stories in the book. When higher personal awareness is achieved, it especially helps expand our connections with those around us, deepening our relationships and our compassion. It is rare and comforting sort of encouragement and support on our spiritual journeys when we discover parallels, or synchronicities experienced.

At whatever point in life you find yourself, with ultra-sensory meditation you can delve into all your spiritual curiosities. Let's get started!

Part One

Defining Ultra-Senses

IT IS COMMON TO HEAR SOMEONE TALK ABOUT HAVING A GUT instinct about a situation. Maybe you, yourself, have driven a new route because you got a sinking feeling or a pit in your stomach about taking your routine course, only to find out later that an accident had occurred there. Perhaps you have heard a noise or have seen a moving shadow that had no apparent source. Or, maybe you had planned to make a pot roast with vegetables for dinner, deciding at the last minute to pick up a pizza on your way from work; then you arrive home to your child declaring he had been hoping for pizza (and apparently bombarding you with that wily telepathic message) all day long. These are ultra-sensory experiences at the most basic and natural level, much as peripheral vision is a foundation-level protection to us, a survival function. At a higher level—one of conscious application—we use our developed ultra-senses to perceive detailed and accurate insights through meditation.

The trouble encountered when starting to pursue meditation and spiritual development is that with the multitude of topics, it can be overwhelming and confusing with so many terms and concepts to understand. What some people think of as intuition, others call their psychic abilities. Do they all mean the same thing? Is any term truly accurate? Intuition, *Merriam-Webster's Online Dictionary* defines as, "the power or faculty of attaining to direct knowledge or cognition without evident rational thought or inference," but where does this *power* come from? If it is a faculty, an *ability*, it could be deduced, too, that not all people are *able* or capable of it, since no one ever has the exact same abilities.

Further confusing is the phrase *extrasensory perception,* ESP, which according to many sources is, "the power to perceive things that are not present to the senses." Is it an extra power certain privileged people have? The prefix *extra* alone implies that it is additional or supplementary, especially if it is as it suggests—*separate* from your senses. All these terms and concepts make trying to comprehend more bewildering, with nothing accurate enough to clarify the experiences. Most of us consider ourselves quite ordinary, intelligent, and logical beings, certainly not bypassing of reason, rational thought, and healthy skepticism, so to make the leap from having a feeling about an occurrence to having psychic ability is implausible. When we struggle with understanding how all these concepts relate to us personally, it is a lot easier to slap a label like intuition on those moments we cannot fully explain, and to quit trying to figure out how it all works.

For the whole of my life, even before I had a full comprehension or name for her, I have been connected to and aware of my spirit guide, my lifetime guide. As I learned to communicate with her over time, she cleared up a lot of my confusion and taught me about numerous spiritual concepts. One significant moment being the day when she explained, it would be more accurate to think of my experiences and of how I perceive information as *ultra-sensory*. Guide or no, human-me wanted to know exactly why she was using that term. I grabbed my *Webster's New Collegiate Dictionary* and looked it up: "Ultra: beyond the range or limits of; beyond what is ordinary, proper, or moderate." *Limit* is the key word. If what we are attempting to recognize are sights, sounds, and information vibrating at a frequency accelerated beyond what our physical senses can measure or perceive, then technically, by extending that scope of perception and removing those limits it should enable us to perceive a higher level of information around us.

Even within the range of our physical senses, we have these occurrences of varied perception. For example, if a car is still, you can clearly see the design of the hubcap on the wheel, but while the car is in motion, the faster it speeds up, though you know there is a design, you can distinguish little to no visible details. As another example, let's say you leave a bottle of ammonia sitting open on the kitchen counter; you can clearly smell this while you are standing in the kitchen and even if you walk into an adjacent room the aroma is lingering, but from two or three rooms away, are you still able to distinguish the smell? You know it is still there. Your perception by sense of smell is dependent on where your physical sense becomes limited. It has nothing to do with you not being able to smell any longer, even if it was something as intense as ammonia.

After all her explaining, my spirit guide made the point clear: our sensory, *ultra-sensory,* acuity is not separate ability, not extra gifts. It is merely a matter of our perception, limited by our dense, slowly vibrating human, physical body. By removing limits of the dense and physical, it enables us to perceive in a heightened manner, at a higher frequency or vibration...beyond the range of usual physical senses. We are not dealing with individual facets, but rather a spectrum of perception. Our commonly recognized physical senses, as human beings, compose one end of that spectrum. It all finally clicked together for me as she explained this. We are all spiritual beings, as such, our soul is our purest form, and therefore, it is our truest nature to perceive information at these higher frequencies. Our dense and physical human form, is what slows us down and essentially causes these limitations to what we are able to discern—to see, feel, hear, smell, taste, and know.

At some point, you have heard someone exclaim, "Everyone is psychic." Although the intention may be earnest on some level, without explanation it is rather unhelpful. More accurately, it should be said that everyone is a spiritual, ultra-sensory being. For that reason, we are all capable of tapping into our soul's natural, ultra-sensory abilities. To whatever extent we choose, we have a right to develop our spiritual awareness. Granted, not all individuals will excel to the same degree with their intuited or ultra-sensory experiences; much like not every person who plays piano will become a world-renown pianist. To great extent, the ultra-sensory experience differs individually and according to each life path and purpose. When it comes to ultra-senses and attaining ultra-sensory awareness on a higher level, people practice and sharpen their own skills, at their own level, for their own purposes, within the boundaries of their own personal evolution. As much as some like to trumpet about how extraordinarily intuitive or sensitive they are; if they were, they simply would *be*. There is no contest. There is no singular, definitive goal, beyond self-awareness.

As a side note, one's spiritual awareness in this lifetime is not a measurement or an excuse to judge against those people who never accept these concepts. Some souls come into their lives with a strict intention not to be raised in a faith-based environment or not to have easily accessible resources or opportunities one needs to achieve heightened spirituality. Perhaps that being wishes to learn if a person can reach spiritual awareness without such parameters. It is not for us to dwell on, but for understanding. If a soul knew that spirituality (or any other personal attribute) could hinder what goals he had, what he wanted to experience, or what challenges he wanted to face during the course of his life, he might be born into and put himself under very different circumstances than what another individual has. Again, this is some, not all. Your soul has done the same for you in setting up your own personal life plan with concepts and challenges that you undertake. Every individual's journey, purpose, or life plan is uniquely their own. It is equally wise to respect the paths of those you do not relate to, as much as those you do.

Having taught workshops over the years to assist people in recognizing their spiritual abilities, I have learned so much about human beings. One realization is that everyone has had ultra-sensory experiences before, but people simply do not recognize them as such. Oftentimes, a group discussion during one of my classes is the first opportunity a person has that brings to light an understanding of these events. As it was for me and for countless others, however the insight or happening comes to you is your own personal measurement of *normal*. After all, the basis to perceiving these experiences is merely the extension of your physical senses; parameters that your soul decided are necessary and appropriate for you in this lifetime.

When we examine the spectrum of each sense individually, it enables us to recognize how we personally process information. This is often the exact moment the recognition begins to unfold that these ultra-sensory events have been going on periodically, perhaps with regularity, over an extended period. Memories from weeks or years prior start to surface. Once inexplicable events now make sense merely by changing perspective on our own perceptions.

By breaking down the whole ultra-sensory experience into individual components, a person can begin to learn which senses happen most naturally, are strongest, or easiest to rely upon initially. The key factor is having an opportunity to study this range of senses and to heighten your own self-awareness. Familiarize yourself with your own senses and abilities, sense-by-sense, working through each of the four steps that follow.

SEEING

The majority of individuals who meditate rely primarily on their ultra-sense of seeing (clairvoyance) to move through the experience and to gain the information or understanding sought from the session. It is typical, when a person is beginning with meditation, for it to be challenging to hold onto an image or scene for an extended stretch, even if you are able to see mental images easily or clearly at other times.

If you have trouble concentrating on images you see in your head (visualizing), beginning with brief meditations is ideal. This way you can increase your confidence and ability to stay in the same state of attentiveness for gradually longer periods. Meditations that you can build upon, or ones that center on simple relaxation, are helpful for starting out. Keep in mind that what you are working with is energy, which is not going to be at a constant, but tends to be fluctuating and fluid. When an image is fading, rather than thinking you have broken out of your relaxed state of consciousness and that you have been unsuccessful, give yourself a chance to remain calm, allowing for that vision or a new image to clearly sharpen. With added practice, you will be able to hold your ability to concentrate for longer periods or try more extensive and complex meditations, too.

 STEP ONE: MEDITATION ON COLORS

Use the following *Meditation on Colors* by first reading through the text and then, sitting comfortably, do the exercise as instructed. Intended to be short exercises, the individual steps in this chapter require no longer than five minutes. It is recommended to repeat the steps a few times over the course of a week or more to compare your results. Doing so allows you to experiment with meditating at different hours of the day and in a variety of environments. Trying the steps multiple, brief periods is better than spending twenty or thirty minutes doing each one once. If it feels like it is a strain, it is too long.

The Meditation:

Find a place to sit where you are uninterrupted and at ease for a few minutes. Relax and close your eyes. Simply concentrate on your breathing. Let everything be dark, quiet, and still. As you listen to your breathing, it will become slower and even. This will help you relax more fully.

Imagine you see a tiny, dim sparkle of light out in front of you. Turn your concentration to this now, picture that you draw it toward you, deeper into your mind, until it feels like it is at the center of your head. Allow this to illuminate the darkness. Let your awareness of sight become clear in this peaceful dark place, especially noticing what color or colors you see swirling around you. Watch the colors and their movement, as well as directions or patterns. What do these colors feel like? How do you feel— the same or different as before you began your meditation? Do you have a sense or *knowing* of what these colors mean to you at this moment? Wrap yourself in one or more of the colors. When you are done, come back by sending that original little sparkle away from you. Watch it withdraw and disappear, leaving you once again in that peaceful darkness. You can then turn your thoughts back to your breathing as you "come home" to your physical awareness, opening your eyes when you are ready. Take a few minutes to write a few notes about your *clairvoyant* experience.

Whether for this step or the subsequent ones, you can revisit the individual exercises whenever you wish. While you may want to repeat one or more of them, do not hold expectation over yourself that there is a level of perfection required in order to move ahead in the sequence. It is entirely about the opportunity to learn how you perceive ultra-sensory information and being able to expand upon this from the base results.

HEARING, FEELING

For those people confident that either feeling (clairsentience) or hearing (clairaudience) is much easier than seeing (clairvoyance), do not let this deter you from meditating. With the five physical senses, gauged from person to person, you would find that people tend to have diverse visual, auditory, or sensory tendencies. For example, you have probably heard someone say, "He is a visual learner" or "I am a very tactile person." The same applies to ultra-sensory experiences as well. Simple meditations or development exercises easily reveal an individual's senses that are more advanced. People most strongly clairsentient, who think they never see clairvoyant imagery, can still tell you after doing a meditation what colors things are, what places they are exploring, and what beings of light are with them. If you ask how they are able to perceive these things without clairvoyant images, they will say it is because they *feel* the answers. Now what is wrong with that? Absolutely nothing. No matter the means, the meditations are useful and successful. They still result in acquiring impressions, answers, or guidance the person is seeking.

Clairsentience consists of two aspects of feeling: the physical and the emotional. There is the sense of feeling as it corresponds with the sense of touch, such as, feeling tingly at the back of your neck when you make contact with a certain spirit guide in meditation, or sensing a genuine warmth or pressure on your skin when the guide gives you a hug.

Also encompassed by clairsentience, is the emotional aspect. An example of this is feeling a great wave of joyfulness when you connect to your guide, or experiencing unconditional love that comes from receiving their hug. Essentially, the physical or emotional aspects of feeling that you experience, that do not have a source based in your human environment, are the heightened perceptions of your ultra-sensory *clairsentience*.

Clairaudience, being able to hear at a higher rate of perception, allows for hearing words, voices, sounds, music, chimes, bells, and such that do not have an obvious physical source. This happens for people in two ways. First, it would include noises heard audibly by you, but that others around you do not notice. These seemingly audible sounds may be like a sonic boom to you, yet you notice everyone else is oblivious to it. One of the more common audible clairaudient experiences people have is of hearing someone, oftentimes a spirit guide, saying their name right as they are waking up or falling asleep. Being in a semi-sleep state already sets your level of perception at a different rate, so it can be easier to discern such sounds.

At my home, we have some playful "visitors" that like to practice our clairaudience with us periodically. They call out our name from another room, so we are regularly going to find the other person, having this interaction:

"Yeah? What did you want?"

"What do you mean?"

"You called for me—did you want something?"

"I didn't say anything."

Basically, it is a household game now and from time to time a guest gets pulled into it, too.

Second, clairaudience includes messages "heard" by way of what is considered the *mind's ear*, in a manner of speaking. Words, sounds, or complete messages transmitted by *infused thought* or telepathy fall into this category. For beings in spirit, without physical vocal chords, this is how they communicate with us. Many people who have had this type of clairaudient experience often describe it as having an idea or words pop into their mind. They may not be able to explain it, but they have the feeling it was not sourced from their own line of thought. If you closely mind your own thought process, over time you will notice how infused thoughts interrupt your own. An example would be thinking to oneself, "I wonder what I ought to do to resolve this problem," and suddenly, out of no linear thought pattern of your own, a complete and viable idea comes to mind. Another example is having your attention quickly diverted to a matter that you need to be aware of, for instance, you perceive the thought, "Do not set the jug of detergent on the edge of the dryer, or it will spill." Half the time we still set the container down, it spills, and all we can do is roll our eyes in hindsight, and say "Thank-you" to whoever was trying to be helpful. We grab a sponge and make a mental note that the next time we hope to listen to the advice.

I know that some people jump to fearful assumptions with the talk of hearing voices, but I assure you the experience is quite dissimilar to that of the people who hear voices related to mental health concerns. The words or messages do not come across in the same way. For those people it is a scary, worrisome, and relentless experience. When you are connecting to your spirit guides however, they will not speak in a manner to panic you. They do not chatter at you as a constant distraction. The communication is not something you feel you have to fight against to keep it quiet. There are never words of negativity, or messages of direct or underlying meaning encouraging someone to cause harm to oneself or others. A spirit guide would never instill paranoia and fear, and certainly, their presence is never invasive, insidious, ominous, or threatening. The simplest, most frank way to differentiate is that a spirit guide will respect your free will; it is an absolute. If you ask them to leave, if you ask them to stop speaking, they will. People who suffer from mentally associated health issues will often beg for relief, for the voices to stop or go away—they do not. It is a helpless feeling to sit with someone who suffers in this way. This is not to say that these issues cannot possibly stem from a spiritual or metaphysical place, completely or in part, but they abso-lutely must have skilled and traditional medical support. If you do find that any of these worrisome particulars do apply to yourself or someone close to you, then it is a sign to seek assistance from a professional healthcare provider.

Back to our topic at hand though, our ultra-senses. So often in this world, we are encouraged or even forced to develop and overcome our weaknesses, rather than to perfect our strengths. Consider your ultra-sensory ability. If you continue to enhance your strengths, supporting them with your secondary senses, you will be applying yourself naturally and sincerely. With that in mind, instead of becoming stressed out or trying to force that sense which feels uncomfortable to rely upon, find reassurance and satisfaction in doing your meditations by allowing your stronger senses to lead you to the goal at hand. This allows your less intense senses to fill in the gaps with supporting detail and to develop at their own pace, as you keep checking in with each of your senses, and as you continue to study your full-sensory range. The more accuracy, validation, and confidence you have to build upon, the more all of your senses improve.

For anyone who is primarily relying on clairaudience or clairsentience in doing the meditations in this book, please note that when you are instructed to "Allow your vision to come into focus," it is appropriate to alter the phrase to read, "Allow your clairaudience to come into focus," or "Allow your senses to come into focus." Then, proceed with the meditation, naturally utilizing your stronger ultra-senses, and allowing the lesser senses to cultivate little by little.

STEP TWO: MEDITATION ON SOUND

As with Step One, first read through the Meditation on Sound a time or two. When you are content in remembering it, begin the exercise.

The Meditation:

Go into meditative state by relaxing, closing your eyes, and listening to your breathing. Feel the gentle rhythm, in and out, relaxing you further as your breathing slows and steadies. Let everything be dark, quiet, and still.

Now let your awareness of sound intensify in this peaceful dark place, being mindful of the sounds you hear around you. Listen for simple noises. Note rhythms or patterns to the sounds. What do the sounds feel like? How do you feel (the same or different as before you began your meditation)? Do you have a sense, or *knowing* of what these sounds mean to you at this moment? Do you perceive specific words, musical notes, or nature sounds? Allow the sounds you choose to blend with your energy. Finish by writing a few notes about your *clairaudient* experience in your journal.

STEP THREE: MEDITATION ON TOUCH & EMOTION

Let yourself consciously relax into a state of serenity and darkness. To more easily center on your sense of touch, keep your eyes closed. Imagine that you sit with your open hands held together out in front of you, palms up. A small, sensory token of some sort is placed in them. Feel the size, shape, and texture of this token. By your sense of touch, without using your meditative sight, are you able to distinguish what the little gift is? Is your token a coin, stone, flower, small animal or another item altogether? Through this process, realize the feelings and emotions you experience, too. Discovering what the token is, who presented it to you, or what the meaning behind it is, can elicit emotional, clairsentient responses as well. Once you have worked through your perceptions of touch and emotion, you may use your clairvoyance and clairaudience to confirm what you felt. Conclude with an expression of gratitude and spend a few minutes journaling about your *clairsentient* experience.

TASTING, SMELLING

The most overlooked ultra-senses are those of taste and smell. Correctly, these are referred to as clairgustance (clear tasting), or clairolience (clear smelling). It is peculiar they are disregarded, if for the sole reason that these are the most easily verifiable ultra-sensory experiences. For example, you suddenly have a strong taste of citrus in your mouth, and pondering this you recognize it as tangerine specifically, yet you have not been eating tangerines. Furthermore, you do not even happen to have any on hand nearby you, and no person within a reasonable distance is eating citrus fruit, so you know it is not a "taste-triggered-by-smell" occurrence. This flavorful experience is coming from somewhere. Once you have ruled out the obvious, then most certainly it is an ultra-sensory event. Among other possible explanations, it could be a telepathic perception, a spirit guide, or passed loved one influencing the message via your taste buds through clairgustance.

The same happens very frequently with smells. With a little rational investigation, it does not take long to discover that a passed loved one, known for her thriving rose garden, has sent the strong smell of roses. Our ultra-senses work for more present purposes too, such as realizing that the smoke smell that fills the room for a flash of an instant was alerting you to a phone call coming from a cigar-aficionado uncle a moment later.

Sometimes we alert to ultra-sensory smells and tastes that do not have immediate validation, yet we find the true significance or message when it follows awhile later. Perhaps understanding arrives through a greater synchronicity, but as long as you can reason out the possibility for a physical and present source, you can always make a note of the circumstances until you get your confirmation.

KNOWING

Lastly, there is the "sixth sense," claircognizance (clear knowing). This is the sense most difficult to explain, yet perhaps the most universally occurring for people. If we consider the most human aspects of how we know things, we think of ideas such as mental reasoning, analytical thinking, or even pure logic. With claircognizance, it comes down wholly to knowing. Knowing without analyzing. Realizing in a moment that an idea is presented that it simply *is*. Many people, when they consciously recognize the experience, refer to a claircognizant event as an "aha moment." Those moments tend to coincide with big notions...solutions to problems, creative thoughts, inventive concepts, quantum theories, reincarnation, the absence of time on the other side, and other spiritual ideas.

What comes after? A student once told me it had been a very long while since having an "aha moment," a revelation of a basic, universal truth. These rudimentary, root concepts may be finite, at least within the parameters of our human limitations. What follows for us, if we want to continue to broaden understanding and explore, are those claircognizant moments that are even more magical, awe-inspiring, and rather than within bold fundamentals, they lie within the subtlest realizations, the tiniest of happenings. If we are widely observational, we will see. These are the moments we access by way of synchronicity or an enlightened experience, or via our claircognizant sense, being able to perceive, to know, our place in the Universe, oneness and our connection to all that is.

With regard to trying to develop your senses, it is always imperative to notice to how you naturally perceive information that comes across to you. Begin to see which ultra-senses are your strongest so you can build upon that foundation, while at the same time trying to tap into and enhance the senses with which you feel less experience or comfort. One recommended way to do this is whenever testing yourself or practicing, attempt to engage a sense that you are more uncertain of first. Then as a secondary measure, use the sense you have more ease with to acquire back up or validating information.

ULTRA-SENSORY PRACTICE GAME

You can try a practice test of your ultra-senses with a game of *"What is on the Checkout Counter?"* Say, for example, that you feel that your psychic sense of smell (clairolience) is weakest, your sense of hearing (clair-audience) is a bit stronger, and your sense of sight (clairvoyance) is your most reliable. Begin this game before you go into the grocery store by attempting to write a list of as many possible items as you can that the person in line ahead of you will put on the checkout counter. Work in a weakest-to-strongest order of how dependable you feel your senses actually are. You would initiate the list by contemplating aromas; maybe you catch a scent of lemon or whiff of fresh bread. Follow this taking a turn with just your clairaudience. What words do you hear when you ask,

"What is on the counter ahead of me?" Perhaps you hear new, additional items like "light bulbs and chicken," or by clairaudience you may hear confirmation that the lemon scent you picked up on is "dish soap." Finally, using your clairvoyance, concentrate on that alone to "see" what is on the counter. When trying to learn to use all your senses reliably, it is much easier and provides a lot more validation for you when you break it down into individual steps, rather than broadly opening up to being bombarded by all of them at once.

As a side note, for those of you going out to try this little game, if you do not have tremendous luck with it, even after a few attempts, do not let that worry you too much. The exercise is entirely about using your ultra-senses in relationship to prediction, or possibly, remote viewing. Not all people have the ability to forecast the future or to view events at a distance of time or space, even with finely tuned senses. Prediction and remote viewing are merely two possible ways perception manifests through a skill and there are numerous alternatives.

On the other hand, if you *do* have great success with this, you will want to try other challenges of prediction or remote viewing to see if your ultra-senses are enabling these abilities for you.

 STEP FOUR:
FESTIVAL for the SENSES MEDITATION

To put all your sensory abilities to use, here is an entertaining meditation to practice discerning each separate sense. It will help to further identify how you perceive information and insights. As well, it can help you to discover which senses come more naturally to you, and which ones require a little more concentration or effort to become aware of initially.

Relax as you begin your meditation. The calm and quiet darkness smoothly gives way to an outdoor setting where the place you find yourself walking comes to some sort of gated, festival event. Pick up your admission ticket from the booth and proceed to walk through the gates. As you do this, concentrate on your clairvoyant sense (sight). Visually take in all that you can for those first steps into the festival. You will quickly learn what kind of event is taking place; see the colors, people, activity, and the environment.

Settling upon a place where you can stop for a moment and feel content, allow yourself to close your eyes on the scene around you so that you can deliberate intently on your clairaudient sense (hearing). Take in all that you can of the activity around you in this way.

When you are satisfied with detecting sounds, open your eyes again on the setting and walk about. This time shift your awareness to all that you feel around you. First, regard physical sensations, such as temperature, or a breeze, warm sun shining down, or rain, if that happens to be the case. Second, take into account the emotions of being at this festival.

Having applied those three significant senses, next you will look to find some sort of food vendor nearby. When you do, order an item or two so that you can practice your clairolience and clairgustance (senses of smell and taste).

This leaves you to test your sense of claircognizance. To do this, search for the old-fashioned fortuneteller cabinet somewhere on the festival grounds. When you press the button to receive your fortune card, anticipate *knowing* your message as you take it from the machine; you may also use your other senses to double check what it says.

Once you have your message you are free to finish or to explore further, but either way, when you are ready to quit, effortlessly wind your way back to the front gates you originally entered through, and as you walk back out past the ticket booth allow the setting to fade behind you.

For Your Journal

Following every meditation throughout the book is a section called "For Your Journal." To help you get even more out of the meditation process, this section presents a bulleted list of several key questions or related ideas pertaining to the meditation that precedes it. Reflect on them as you record your meditative experiences. Let your inner voice guide you through answering the questions.

Journaling allows for thoughtful contemplation of the experience. It is a time to assess and recognize the meanings behind the symbolism and messages, and a way to analyze the insights and information received so that you can continue to apply what you discover beyond the few minutes spent in meditation. Getting in the habit of writing these experiences down in a journal creates an organized reference. Sometimes, going back when you are feeling more distanced from a situation or when you have gained more insights from day-to-day, can help you with clarity on an issue or the intent of a meditation.

Often, the timing of doing your meditation is midway through a sequence of meaningful life events, and being able to look back on what you have written is quite helpful in putting all the pieces together in hindsight. Years from now, it is probable that you will find value in having this collection of your own personal stories to look back on, sometimes for validation, sometimes for the sake of memory, and sometimes to be able to see how far you have come. Ultimately, the combination of meditation and journaling help us to deepen understanding of our life paths and to know ourselves. This leads us toward fulfillment on our journeys as a whole.

○ Regarding the festival meditation, write the story of how the process flowed, including all you saw, heard, felt, smelled, or tasted.

○ Which senses came easiest to you? Was there a specific sense you used that took a little longer to grasp?

○ Record the message you received at the end (via claircognizance).

○ Detail significant aspects about the type of festival or about what you encountered there. Consider if these hold any personal meaning for you. For example, a familiar place may emphasize nostalgic moments and those with whom you enjoyed that occasion. A food you have never tried, but always hoped to, may be a nudge for you to pursue life's little indulgences.

Taking time to reflect on your sensory perceptions in this way is more than the average person will ever bother to do, so you have made a big step toward elevating your awareness already. It assuredly grows more effortless. Keep up the good work!

MADAME ZELDA
Heather

In class, I was doing a meditation along with my students about being at a festival. Horror of horrors. I get where I was going, fully expecting it is going to be this fantastic renaissance-type ambience, or at minimum enjoyable, only to find I am greeted at the gates by this most awful 20-foot-clown-man-on-stilts complete with red and white striped pants and a gargantuan blow-up head. I thought this might be the longest fifteen minutes of my life. If you have a touch of coulrophobia, you understand me.

The rest of the journey was proving unsettling and loud — people, animals, and commotion. Chattering pre-teens talked about Spice Girls and a mother scolded little boys, "Get down from there, you are not supposed to climb on that!" Somehow, I had to get through this to the end of the meditation, which was nothing short of funny or cliché in itself.

Way in the back corner of this carnival was an old, freight train caboose labeled for the occasion, Madame Zelda. *She was waiting for me on its steps. To share a clear impression of her, she was a cross between a distant relative and a woman I worked with for a summer stint in a fragrance and cosmetics depart-ment. Like the former, she had jet-black dyed hair done up in a helmet of a beehive, black penciled-on eyebrows, candy-apple red lipstick, and long press-on nails. Similar to the latter, she was a straight-forward woman with the raspiest smoker's voice, who called everyone Honey. So, Madame Zelda oh-honey's-me, then gives me a message and a card with a picture on it. I knew right away that it was regarding a friendship that I was struggling with at the time. Feeling like that was the end of my exchange with Madame Zelda I left quickly.*

I found myself finished with the meditation, thinking, "that was odd," when it occurred to me that if I had gone somewhere I had wanted to go to, somewhere remotely appealing to me, I may have thought it was somewhere of my own creation or imagination. This place I would not have chosen on my own in, well, ever. I also would not have believed the message she gave me because what she said was a validation for a soul agreement I was having a hard time understanding in the first place. The way it all played out, I guess I ought to give the Universe the benefit of the doubt; try to have a little faith in the message...and in my higher self.

VISUALIZATION vs. MEDITATION

When fully trying to understand applying your ultra-senses for successful meditation, it is also helpful to recognize the difference between visualization and meditation. Though similar and complementary, they are still separate skills.

Visualization, a mental imagery technique best made known by Shakti Gawain, is the practice of utilizing your ultra-sense of clairvoyance, primarily, to envision a scenario in your mind with the set intention to generate a distinct result. Various possibilities exist for application of the process, such as healing, creating desired outcomes, or manifesting your needs fulfilled.

If I tell you, "Imagine a golden dog," what impression comes to your mind? That dog you have purposely intended to picture is your visualization. Of course, you can use visualization in more complex ways. Take a favorite sports figure as an example; think back to an instance you were watching them perform, or take notice the next time you see them. Witness them using the skill of visualization to help them achieve their goal of shooting that free throw or sinking that putt. Watch the Olympic swimmer as he sits before a meet intently staring at the lane ahead of him, visualizing each stroke as he wishes his race to evolve, second by fraction of a second.

Have you used visualization without even realizing it? Perhaps prior to a meeting with your boss, you have imagined that it results in the offer of a raise. Maybe you have seen in your mind's eye that your friend will be ecstatic upon opening her birthday gift while you are buying it. Or possibly, you have pictured how your room makeover would look when it was finished. All these types of moments are natural uses of visualization. To clarify, visualization is that part of *seeing* which you have set intention over — the pieces that you want and are choosing to imagine, usually with some desire for the outcome to manifest as a reality.

There is a fine line between visualization and meditation, and that line is the intent. It is the instruction versus the communication. Visualization turns to meditation, which is the *communication* part of the experience, when you begin to perceive details, scenes, or completely involved events, of which you had no prior plan or vision. You may have set an intention to gain insights or guidance on a precise theme at the start of your meditation, but without knowing what information will come to you. At the point where visualization bridges into meditation — perception of the *mind's eye* — insights come from another source. A spirit guide, a passed loved one, an angel, the Universal Mind, All That Is, God (by whatever name you call Him), or your higher self, are all possible sources. Being in an altered, more highly vibrating, or highly attuned state of consciousness, enables you to communicate at a greater level, potentially aligned with your whole spirit.

Think quickly back to the golden dog for a moment. Can you describe the dog you see? Now imagine the dog, regardless of your initial perception, stands and begins to walk toward a thing or place. Follow along by watching in your mind's eye (your clairvoyance at work) where the golden dog goes. This is the idea of meditation vs. visualization. The visualization is the suggestion of a golden dog, standing, walking, to something or some place. The meditation part includes the very individualized perception you have of the dog, to where and to what you see the dog walk. All the details, the blanks, filled-in by these other sources, from your own subconscious, your higher self and beyond.

Three different people tried the exercise; all began with instructions of the exact visualization you have been given suggestion of above. The description of their experiences demonstrates that where the intent falls away, the scene shifts into meditation where the individualized, significant factors evolve. These are the results:

Person One: *"I saw a golden retriever. She stood up and walked through a field of tall grass, up to an orange that was lying on a patch of matted-down grass. There was a black bird with red and blue markings and a longer, curved beak sitting on the orange. The bird looked to be guarding the orange."*

Person Two: *"I saw a small dog with sparkly, shining glitter all around it. The dog was alive and jumping and when it jumped, the glitter would fly off its fur. It walked toward my right and went into a building with a big door. I also saw it had a collar with a tag that was gold in color and that had an inscription, but I did not read it."*

Person Three: *"The dog I saw was a giant golden statue, much like you would see an ancient Egyptian cat portrayed. Very stylized, thin, and tall, with sharp, angled eyes, but rather than a cat, it was a dog, with ears more like a beagle. To stand, the statue came to life, walked ahead crossing through a small river, or maybe it was a large river, since the statue was exceptionally tall. On the opposite bank was a grove of trees to the right. The dog appeared as tall as the trees, and he went toward the left and lay down in an open meadow at the edge of a cliff to watch the coral sunset."*

You can see for yourself how the suggested visualization of the dog came to life through each person's own personal meditation. If they had set an intention to answer a question beforehand, chances are that the symbolism would have provided insights in support of answering that question, too.

THE MEDITATIVE PROCESS

When it comes to learning meditation, everyone must start somewhere. When I tried (and tried, and tried again) to learn to meditate, based on nothing at first, besides my own assumptions and the unfortunate advice I heard somewhere to "clear your mind," the results were as you imagine, not too successful. Every time I sat and tried to force myself to not think, I ended up filtering through a to-do list, thinking of an e-mail I forgot to send earlier, or having some other distraction interfere. If not that, exhaustion from trying to figure out what was supposed to happen would set in and I would fall asleep. Now I am the first to acknowledge that one of the key purposes for meditation *is* in fact relaxation, sleep-state being about as relaxed as one can be, but this was entirely aggravating. Falling asleep sitting up and waking to the agony of a crick in the neck is not ideal. I sure did not feel that I was having success achieving great revelations, let alone gaining useful pointers for the day ahead.

The fundamental problem? If a person is commanding the void of an "empty mind," in fact, all he is doing is preventing insights and information from ever arriving. A meditative mind is quite active—peaceful and still, of course, but most certainly, engaged.

Regarding those to-do lists, if they are the first impressions that surface, it is okay. Allow yourself a chance to arrange them in your thoughts. Once you grant yourself this aside, relax, and carry on with your meditation. On the occasion that the entire takeaway is organizing some daily priorities, which in turn, gives you peace of mind for the day ahead, technically the meditation has worked. Even when it goes against your expectation, it has helped. Your higher self does look out for you.

Also, do not be deterred by stringent advice. Years ago, one author I was reading on an altogether different subject, mentioned it was crucial to meditate at the same time every day, for at least an hour. A second one suggested that meditating in short bursts at least ten times per day is better than meditating for a full hour. Another advised a formula of writing, praying, and meditating that added up to six hours per day. How realistic is that to anyone in this hectic, modern world? Perhaps those plans worked for those individuals, but when trying to incorporate meditation into a life, into an already demanding daily routine, people need a practical solution. One that will not be abandoned before it has begun. Feeling obligated or distracted deters a person from trying to learn. We all should be encouraged to find a flexible formula that works for us, and for our own schedules, needs, and goals.

When it finally sank in that I should ask my spirit guide to teach me, she began to show me that I could meditate at any time, for any length of time, anywhere, and under whatever circumstances I chose. This was a relief and joyful breakthrough. Sometimes you do have the chance to set a perfect mood with nice music or nature sounds playing in the background of a room dimly lit by candles, but oftentimes you do not. Lie down, sit in a chair, kneel or sit cross-legged on a yoga mat, play music, have absolute silence, turn off all the lights, be outside in the full, bright sun. Find space of your own in a noisy, crowded place. Specifics in ambiance are secondary. As long as *you* feel comfortable and inspired, that is when and where you ought to meditate.

A few of my students could tell you stories of how irritated they have been with me because I asked them to do a meditation, quite deliberately having changed the lighting, the music, or the ambience in some way from what they were growing accustomed to during previous classes. Conditioning ourselves to a solitary scenario for our meditative experience develops a dependency on it. Flexibility is a caution against that dependence. Whether it is the chair you sit in, or the candles you light, it will benefit you to be a little less predictable. We, alone, are responsible for convincing ourselves that we cannot possibly meditate in unfamiliar circumstances.

What would happen if you could *only* concentrate on your job while sitting in one specific chair, with a blue gel-ink pen wedged over your left ear, facing a northeasterly direction? How productive would you be if you were called into a meeting room two floors up to present your revolutionary new idea to other associates? Would you carry your chair along with you? I am not suggesting you re-invent your meditation routine every time—there is inherent calmness in habit, certainly—but once you get a feel for the meditation process, go ahead, and change the scenery sporadically. Know that you can meditate when-ever and wherever you need. It will work, because you have not set limitations on yourself. Train yourself to practice with variance. That way you can access peace and relaxation whenever you need. If you want healing or guidance, you will not have to wait. The options are countless.

While I was learning meditation, in recognizing that a singular way is not necessary, I no longer found myself discouraged, or falling asleep, or left with zero insights and the guilt that I could have spent my wasted time elsewhere.

After a period of miscues, attempts, and neck-cricks, in the end, this is how I was taught to meditate, with my guide introducing a starting point or a scene for me to visualize, and then continuing along from there. Focusing on that instructed, intended visualization gives a point on which to concentrate. Directing your physical senses allows their extension—your ultra-sensory abilities—to take effect as you continue to focus.

The best description I ever have heard for meditation is *conscious relaxation*. As with the golden dog exercise, your senses logically center on the dog that you visualize. Then, you naturally begin to relax deliberately into a higher state of awareness, your meditative state. Of course, a longer meditation, under your most personally ideal conditions and an uninterrupted personal space, may yield the best results, but it is truly not vital. In fact, it is nice to take a meditation break in a noisy cafe surrounded by people; with eyes open, no one even suspects.

BUTTERFLY HEALING MEDITATION

Sitting at work on a stressful day, a meditation is a pleasant respite. As brief as thirty seconds, it is a perfect way to mentally recharge and re-tune. You can try it right now. All you need to do is sit still, eyes fixed on blank, unmoving space. Become aware of your breathing, and then visualize a butterfly emerging from a cocoon. Concentrate on the brilliant color of this butterfly and watch as it begins to fly, spiraling around you, leaving a trail of this same colorful light to gently wrap you in its healing energy. Return your attention to your breathing and exhale deeply to release all unwanted energy.

That is the whole of it. What color are the butterfly and the light? Were you in need of healing? You may have seen a green light. Were you merely hoping to relax for a moment? Perhaps you saw a peaceful pale pink or blue. If you were upset when you began, then you may have seen a joyful yellow light. Whatever color it is that you see in the meditation, the boost of that distinct light energy will help you find your center of balance. Colors are an important part of meditations, and you will find several that intentionally play on color throughout the book.

DIVERSIONS

Regarding the challenges of meditation, one of the most common struggles for people who are new to meditation is the concentration factor. This often is the result of the thought process remaining at a superficial level. When you are going through your initial steps of relaxation, as your level of awareness heightens, pay attention for a literal, physical feeling of the thoughts or images moving back further into your head, more above the ears, or to the center-top of your head, rather than just behind your forehead.

To experience this for yourself before you begin your next meditation, think of this short shopping list: avocados, apples, bagels, and cashews. Do you notice how the thought or imagery literally feels like it is at the front of your mind? Now when you go to do your meditation, become aware of how these initial sensory impressions gradually shift deeper into your head and consciousness, the more relaxed and meditative you become. When you feel like this, as though you perceive your ultra-senses from the center of your mind, then you will know you are in a place of insightful concentration.

Every so often, I have a student who says he is having trouble following along with a guided meditation, in that he visualized information or settings other than what the original instruction suggested. Should you experience that situation, I would not worry too much about it. Even when following a descriptive visualization, a little detour toward accessing information or insights in your own way is a periodic likelihood. If you feel peaceful in your meditation and you know that you can communicate to ask questions, you are going to get results out of the session.

Now, if this drifting happens consistently, try to reconsider how you are opening your meditation sessions; perhaps the intention you are setting is vague or not well worded. Ask yourself if you are resistant to some compo-nent of the experience, or are approaching the meditation with any manner of fear. Having that added self-awareness and addressing it will help you to continue.

Furthermore, diversions may arise in the midst of a meditation. If it is of importance that you accomplish a task within the course of a meditation and something is standing in your way of completing it, try to ascertain what is obstructing you from proceeding. Ask yourself reflective questions to get to the source of the dilemma. Honest answers tend to resolve obstacles.

As an example, I guided a meditation where everyone was to unlock a door. Entering the building led to an opportunity to release a fear. Following the meditation, one woman said that despite what she tried, she was unable to unlock the door. It is her meditation, her doorway. The blockage impeding her meditation is hers as well. The answer as to why this was happening was for her to realize. Was it a question of not being ready to let go of her fear? Was it a matter of it not being the right timing for her to resolve this issue? Was there something about the fear that she was, as of yet, unwilling to face? She alone holds the answer and the ability to decide when and how to move forward in the meditation. If you ever happen to experience a similar circumstance, finish with your meditation, take a little time to think honestly about what is holding you back, and you can always do the meditation again later. Trying to force a meditation to progress could be frustrating and unrewarding. It could also prove inaccurate, if you were to make yourself see no more than what you want to see.

Starting out, think of the meditation learning process as an old attic, where belongings have been stored for as many years as you are old. The mental clutter needs clearing and sorting in an initial phase of meditation attempts, in order to achieve a modicum of balance, peace, and clarity. We accomplish this by continuing to develop self-awareness through repetition of endeavors. Once the "attic" is organized, falling into meditative state becomes progressively effortless. Until then, during the beginning phase, it only makes sense for it to be a bit of an upheaval, haphazard and unpredictable. In other words, erratic is normal at first. Be kind to yourself, and try the meditation another day.

GUIDED
Carol S.

This occurred multiple times throughout taking Heather's beginning workshops and for a while afterward. During the meditations, I would see a host of heads, *starting with the larger ones in front and getting smaller as they progressed into the background. The odd thing was that all these heads appeared to be a faceless, soft, gentle shade of white.*

The faces were not frightening nor were they unknown. They all were familiar to me and were loving and comforting. After a few weeks, my hosts *disappeared, but I was left with a stronger sense of self and a sense of comfort. They were exactly what I needed at the time. Their messages to me were about self-worth and trusting myself. Thank you, my loving, faceless friends.*

Part Two

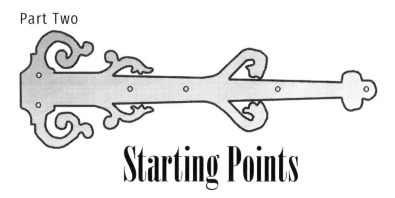

Starting Points

> *"Meditation is the life of virtue, as virtue is the life of the soul. It is the conduit by which a happy and delightful communication is maintained between God and the soul; through which the graces and blessings of God descend to the soul, and through which the ardour, the praises, and adoration of the soul, ascend to God."*

-*Wellins Calcott*, Thoughts Moral and Divine

USING A CONSISTENT STARTING POINT FOR MEDITATION IS beneficial, especially as a beginner, but also for someone adept at meditation when trying to meditate at a stressful or anxious time. When you know where you are going to go beforehand, it provides comfort. This allows you to relax and open up to what is important to see, feel, hear, and learn, as you launch beyond your opening scene into any of the meditative experiences.

One of the starting points for several of the meditations you will find in this book is *The Hallway* meditation that follows. Once you have completed that basic meditation, *Your Personal Space* meditation should be your second meditative journey, which ultimately you should consider your go-to meditation. It is truly a foundation for your meditative experiences, as it is a wholly sacred, safe, relaxing, and a soon familiar scene in which to reflect. If ever you find yourself lacking time to learn a new meditation, or if you feel you are having difficulty relaxing or concentrating, *Your Personal Space* is ready for you and is adaptable for every occasion. You will find healing, guidance, and wisdom there whenever you need it.

A number of the meditations incorporate the outdoors and aspects of nature; several have paths, trails, and park or garden settings. As you have undoubtedly experienced on your own, whether going for a run, hiking a trail, planting your spring garden, or sitting on a beach somewhere, being outside and connecting with Mother Nature is restorative, soothing, and healing. When we venture outdoors with a reflective and observational mindset, Nature embraces us and teaches us how to be still.

Gardens are idyllic spaces with a capacity to transcend time and turmoil. They exemplify energy of growth, renewal, creativity, and fertility. Nature parallels our objectives for meditation, making it an ideal backdrop in most instances. Unquestionably, it benefits us to devote time to explore the outdoors whenever possible. Often-times however, when you find the chance to meditate, you may not have the option be outdoors to take advantage of nature's transformative qualities, so these meditation settings are one clever way of bringing nature instantly to you, wherever you happen to be.

USING THIS BOOK

Aside from beginning with the sensory meditations in Part One and the starting point meditations that are yet to follow in Part Two, there is no pre-determined order for doing the meditations. There is no requirement or expectation, no formula for right or wrong. Try the meditations whenever, wherever, and in whatever order you feel drawn to use them. They are now resources for those times you need them and want to enjoy them.

One main factor to be aware of regarding the order of the meditations and that is those appearing first, sequentially, do not reference working with your spirit guides. Then, on pages 149, 155, and 159, three separate meditations present opportunities to meet your highest guide, healing guide, and an animal guide, if you opt to use them. The meditations that follow those three more purposefully allow for interaction with these spirit helpers. It is just a note to be aware of when making your selections. (Of course, every now and then, a spirit guide appears in a meditation where you are not specifically intent on working with them anyway. It is almost as if they are here to support and guide us.)

Some of the meditations you will enjoy greatly, often repeating your favorites. Another one you use for a specific purpose or concern and then you do not need it again for a while. Another is a favorite of a friend, yet you do not find a need for it at the same time. One you pass up thinking it is not meant for you, then a certain event occurs in life and suddenly your mind is set on trying it. Trust your inner voice in choosing the right meditations at the best time for *you*.

An alphabetical Index of Meditations (page 258) is followed by an Index of Meditations by Purpose and Need (page 261). When you want to meditate for a specific reason or if you are looking for a certain theme, refer to this, as the groupings will aid in finding one that suits the moment.

Additionally, theme icons (shown on the following page) caption each meditation title page. Use them as a guide when selecting a meditation of interest. It is good to note that only the seven most common themes have icons, while the complete index denotes a broad range of additional categories.

If ever there is a time you feel uncertain as to which meditation to try or what it is that you need most, you can still find the best option. Use this quick *bibliomancy* (divination using a book) exercise to help you choose. Simply hold on to the book as you think to yourself, "Which meditation is best for me in this moment?" Then, open the book to a random page and try the meditation shown. Remember, it is *your* spiritual journey and you *know* your way.

ICON KEY:

 Decisions, making choices

 Exploration, discovery

 Healing

 Understanding

 Messages, guidance, advice, answers, information, insights

 Spiritual and personal growth, wisdom, higher awareness

 Change, breaking cycles, removing blockages

ENTERING MEDITATIVE STATE

The first paragraph of *The Hallway* meditation that follows is the best routine to use as a foundation for all your meditations. While being flexible with your ambiance is important, an established opening routine is more so. It sets intention and cues your mind that you are ready to meditate. Rather than to repeat the introduction process for every entry in this book, it is written here once and is highlighted for this reason. Be sure to bookmark the page for easy referencing. Read on and try *The Hallway* meditation, then continue the practice as you proceed with others.

The HALLWAY

Begin by allowing yourself to relax. Close your eyes. Relax each part of your body from head to toe, or from your feet to the top of your head, whichever direction feels natural and comfortable to you. Allow all the tension and stress to drain out and away from your body. View yourself as a fluid column of radiant light, firmly anchored to the center of the earth at your feet and connected to all that is from your head and above. This will help you feel balanced, grounded, and protected. Concentrate on your breathing. Listen fully to it. Let the gentle rhythm lull you. See, hear, and feel, while surrounded in silent, peaceful, safe darkness. As you do this, your consciousness drifts into a higher and deeper point of awareness, your meditative state.

When you are feeling relaxed and ready to begin, center your attention on a softly glowing light in the distance. As you bring your vision and senses into focus, you will see that light very faintly illuminates the long and wide hallway. At this point, you need to do nothing more than familiarize yourself with this hallway from where you are standing. As you remain stationary in the hallway, take in what you can see. What does the floor look like? Is it covered or bare? What texture and color are the walls? How do you describe the architecture? How peaceful does it feel? What other sensory impressions arise here?

Try to hold onto your impression of the hallway for ten seconds, thirty seconds, or a minute…as much time as is easy for you, without trying to make it extensive. Intended to be a short visit, *The Hallway* meditation is the first chance to put your ultra-senses to work, practicing fixating on a scene to examine finer detail. Absorb the sensations of this starting point. Once you have done this then let your vision and senses fade into darkness once again. Return your thoughts back to your breathing, while still relaxing and taking your time to finish. For some people it helps to wiggle your fingers and toes, making sure you are physically present, and that your awareness has shifted back to the physical before opening your eyes.

For Your Journal

- Record the answers and details of the questions asked above, describing the hallway that you saw.
- Write your impressions on how you felt going through the meditation.
- How would you describe the atmosphere?
- How long did you spend in meditation this session?

YOUR PERSONAL SPACE MEDITATION

As you practiced with the first paragraph of *The Hallway* meditation, begin by using that same opening relaxation strategy to bring your conscious awareness to a higher state.

Allowing your vision to sharpen, you will find yourself in your familiar, dimly lit hallway. Walk to the first door on the right. Take in the colors, texture, style and other qualities of the door. As you are ready, open it, and pass through the doorway. Do not be startled if it is quite bright. Give your eyes a chance to adjust and welcome the brilliance and warmth of the light surrounding you.

When you are able to see clearly, you find yourself either inside or outdoors. If you are within a room, walk through it to find a door that will bring you outside. Whether it is directly or by passing through the room, once outside you will find a path to follow. Take as much time as you like to enjoy and familiarize yourself with this path. Allow yourself to absorb the sounds, fragrances, and landscape. As you walk along this path, you may find a sense of peace and calm, and even excitement, as you know it is leading you to your personal, private space. You will find that the path comes to a fork. For this meditation, take the path as it leads to the left. There will be a stream for you to go over. As you approach, you will see a foot-bridge or another simple way to cross to the opposite side.

Arriving on the far bank, you find yourself in your personal space. This place is yours and yours alone to come to whenever you wish. It may turn out to be some place you recognize, or it may be completely new to you. Either way, it is a place for reflection, healing, comfort, security, learning, and anything you ever wish it to be. Find a spot to sit, observe, and enjoy yourself. When you are ready to return, follow the same path in reverse to the hallway, closing the door behind you and allowing the imagery to fade away. Do not forget to record your impression and experience.

For Your Journal

○ Describe the door, including its features, style, and colors. In doing so, you will always quickly recognize it as the gateway to your personal space.
○ How did you arrive to the path outside? Was it immediately beyond the door, or did you pass through a room to get there?
○ What details (landscape, sounds, scents) did you distinguish along your walk?
○ What was the emotional atmosphere of this journey?
○ Describe your personal space. Was it a place new to you? Was it somewhere familiar or from your past?
○ What view did you take in as you sat down to observe?
○ Include other feelings, thoughts, or impressions you retain through this experience.
○ How long did you spend meditating? Were you able to maintain impressions for a longer time? With practice, it becomes easier to concentrate for extended periods, as well as to discern sensory insights more clearly.

Everyone who views the first door on the right sees it in a unique and individualized way. So, if you ever compare notes with someone else, do not be alarmed when that person gives an entirely different description than yours.

This is how it ought to be. Even if you hear about similarities to another person's door, be assured that your door is exclusively for you.

MAKE IT YOUR OWN

Once you have tried going into meditative state as described in *The Hallway* a few times, it is an option to customize the opening routine for achieving your meditative state to suit you even better. Some people need a little extra help with reaching that state of concentration. There is nothing wrong with experimenting to find what personally works best.

There are several ideas to consider individually or in combination. Try counting from one to ten along with each breath in and out, with the intention that ten is your highest level of awareness and each number counted brings you one step higher to reach that level. Alternatively, set an intention for yourself that whenever you are sitting, and you rest your open hands on your knees with your palms facing up, that it is signaling that you are an open conduit now connected to meditative state of awareness. Use an affirmation to open your meditation. Say a prayer as you begin your routine. Send a thought inviting your guides or angels to join you. Ask *your* Divine presence (God, Goddess, Buddha, Yahweh, Allah, the Great Spirit, Brahma, Azna, or All That Is) to guide and protect your way. Whatever it is that helps you feel more comfortable and peaceful is going to ease and facilitate your meditations, so feel free to try your own blend until you find an exact routine that works the best for you.

Part Three

The Meditations

"*Another world bloomed around me. I could see the tiniest details. The images were usually very beautiful. One very pleasant thing I remember about these "places" was the feeling that time did not pass while I was there, and I could stay and enjoy them for as long as I wished.*"

- S., from remarks on *Through the Blue Door* meditations

A SPIRITUAL GIFT

The Hallway is the starting point for this meditation (page 56). Go to the second door on the right this time, which will bring you into a room filled with boxes. One box visibly stands out from the rest, despite the many variations in shapes and sizes. It sometimes takes a little rummaging around to find precisely the right one, but feel free to move things as you please. The box you are seeking may be different in that it has your name on it, or it is more ornate, or it could appear identical to the rest except for that you find yourself drawn toward it. Truly, you will know when you have picked the right one.

Open the container and find out what is inside. It is a spiritual gift to you. If you are uncertain of the meaning, listen for messages about your gift as you hold it, or look to see if there is a paper inside the box explaining any symbolism to you. Then, take your new gift with you when you return, going back through the door into the hallway. Close the door behind you and let everything fade as you relax to come back.

For Your Journal

- ◎ Describe the room that contained the boxes.
- ◎ How did you find your box? What made it stand out to you?
- ◎ Inside, what gift did you find?
- ◎ Was there a message given or included in the box?

○ Did you receive the whole gift or a portion of the gift? It is possible for a gift to be shown to you in parts; return visits will enable you to collect all of them to piece it together.

○ What are your thoughts on the gift that you found? Did you have any sort of emotional reaction to it?

○ Sometimes the gift is spiritually insightful. In some instances, it is a reflection of literal, spiritual aspects of your life. Have you had recent signs in your daily life that were indication of such a gift coming to you?

○ Did this provide you with validation immediately?

○ In days to come, see how ideas about how to apply this gift are revealed in your life.

Further journaling:

Write about your personal gifts. What are they? How are you using them? What natural talents or interests have you set aside that you would like to incorporate back into your life? What gifts do other people see in you that you have not recognized yet? Do any of these gifts parallel with or connect to the gift discovered in your meditation?

MESSAGE in a BOX
Holly B.

Although I have been meditating for years, I have always had a difficult time staying in my meditation...my mind has a tendency to wander. After learning to use The Hallway starting point to help me focus, I was able to slip into my meditative state quickly, and to stay focused throughout the time on what I needed to be. I found the descriptive words easy to keep in mind and could imagine myself in my hallway with all of my favorite and comfortable sights, sounds, and smells.

This was an easy meditation to follow, as I was able to continue onward from my hallway to find answers to my questions. By locating the correct door and being able to look through the boxes until my *box presented itself, I was able to receive the guidance that I have been seeking: "Let it sort itself out. Don't try to control it or you will miss the journey and fun." It was in the most uniquely shaped, skinny rectangle box and as soon as I found it in the room, I knew it was the message for me. I have been struggling with several situations in my life that I really want to turn out a certain way. When I turned it over to the Universe and asked for their message, exactly what I needed reminding of, I received. Since this meditation I have been able to enjoy the lessons in my life and trust that they will work out how they are meant to, not only how I expect them to.*

FLOWERBED

As your vision enhances, you will find yourself in an outdoor setting where a raised flowerbed is filled with rich, black soil. You will be able to comfortably position yourself at the side of the flowerbed to plant seeds.

Along the edge of the bed, as you approach, you will find a basket of flower seed packets. Choose two or three kinds that you would like to grow in your garden. Select whichever ones draw you in at the time, even if the choices surprise you. You will discover that each flower variety is representative of a quality that you wish to grow within yourself or of a personal goal.

Take time to plant the seeds, knowing that anytime hereafter, you will be able to return to your flowerbed to care for the flowers, or to do more planting. As you finish your work, step back and take a minute to embrace the emotions and absorb any further information that is important to your growth process here.

When you are ready to come back, close your eyes, and allow everything to fade into peaceful darkness as you become aware of your breathing once again.

For Your Journal

◎ Remember to record the varieties of flowers and the associated qualities, traits, or goals they symbolize.

- Write down a description of your garden bed, and anything else that caught your eye during the experience.
- If you received direct messages, be sure to note those.
- What current events necessitate the qualities or growth you seek?
- What are you hopeful you will manifest in your life, enabled and empowered by having these qualities or growth?
- Use the *Symbolism of Flowers & Trees* (page 277) to see if other important insights or validations surface, regarding the types of flowers you selected.

FACTORY MEDITATION

You are on your way to visit a factory as you begin this meditation. Whether you are immediately inside the building, or must approach and enter from outside, varies from person to person and session to session. In one of my own sessions, I recall starting outside in the distance from a solitary, gray building. Upon arriving to it, I went through a main entrance and was led through the initial visit as part of a tour group. It reminded me of touring the Federal Depository. Contrasting to this, a student found the entire meditation presented as an animation, complete with silly characters, which had never happened to her before. However this opening part of your meditation presents itself to you is completely fine; flow with it and take in as much of the detail as you are able. (If the sign outside says ACME though, keep an eye out for that coyote).

At some point, you will be directed toward a larger, rather open room with conveyor belts running. You can choose a belt to stand aside. Several items will appear along the scrolling belt. Your job will be to sort through the items you wish to keep and those you want to pass on, ultimately, selecting three in total. Sometimes with meditation, it can take a minute to see an object or its details clearly to find out what you truly have in hand. Leave the factory mishaps to Lucy and Ethel, knowing that you can halt the mechanics to have time to think about whether or not to keep or to discard an item before you continue.

Also, you can choose a piece and exchange it for a different one that turns up further down the conveyor that you find more connection to or more appealing, but when you are done you should have your main three items to keep.

While there, in another room of the factory, or upon exiting the building (whichever feels appropriate), carefully consider the individual items you kept. Concentrating on one at a time, ask for messages regarding their importance to you. If you think any of the items you discarded warrant further insights, ask questions about their significance as well. Aside from our partialities, there can be a lot to learn from our aversions, too. Through this process of choosing and exchange, hope to gain understanding of how to be rid of superfluous concerns, beliefs, or situations in life and know how to resolve them so that you can devote yourself to more current ones that need your consideration or action now.

For Your Journal

◎ What are your initial impressions of the factory? Include your ideas about the outer appearance, color, complexity of design, or its building materials. Do you know what kind of factory it is?

◎ What you have noted regarding the significance of symbolism related to the building, whether personal or traditional?

◎ Did you notice or read any signs? Did you receive direction from anyone?

◎ Write about the process of selecting the items from the conveyor belt. Did you trade out any? Which ones were your three keepers?

- Be sure to record the messages and insights you receive about all the items you kept or exchanged, or notable ones that you discarded.
- Overall, what do you think are your dispensable concerns? What aspects of your present or near future deserve your energy?

FOOD for THOUGHT
JoAnn

My factory entrance door was wide-open like an airplane hangar. As many times as I tried to go through the middle or to find a bigger room, I kept going over to the right side into a little office. I was by myself. Initially the conveyor belt was vertical coming down from the ceiling of the room. I could see it through the glass window. Once I entered the room, the belt lowered into a horizontal position and moved right to left. The window and door to the office was behind me. The following items came to me: a chicken breast, toolbox, light bulb, sock, mattress, keys, pen, and pencil. Almost immediately, I became very sleepy and got a headache. I actually fell asleep doing this (for real, not in my meditation). When I woke up returning to the meditation, the conveyor belt had stopped, and I had my three things. I left the small office and went out the big door I had entered.

It felt like there was a huge airplane in the bigger room all the time. Once I stopped fighting wanting to go to into the big room and went into the small office, things happened quickly. Now that I think about it most of the items represented things that I feel I need, am uncomfortable when I do not have them, and feel safer when I have them or at least know where they are at even if I do not use them. Food, *represented by the chicken breast;* keys, *represented the one thing that I am always double-checking because I am always losing them. I am literally stuck without them.* Mattress *represents my sleep. I have narcolepsy. If I am not sleeping well everything in my life is off balance, everything.*

ESCALATOR

Before you get started with your meditation, have a question or topic in mind that you would like information and guidance on during the session.

An escalator is revealed as you begin. Riding on it gently brings you to a higher level. As you step off at the top, choose which of the directions you would like to search for receiving your insights on this subject.

Walking straight ahead will provide information as to the reality of the situation. Here is where to see things as they really are. It is also a place to discover correlating elements that may have been unknown to you previously.

Going off to the left will reveal changes that you can make regarding the topic of your question, for the sake of detaching from it. You can do what is needed so it will no longer be an issue for you. This option is about putting it in the past. It may also show possible outcomes or repercussions.

Turning to the right you will find guidance as to choices available to you or ways to find resolution, betterment, and happiness with the matter at hand. This option is for improving and moving forward; it may demonstrate the potential impacts of these choices.

When you have spent enough time here to find answers or insight on your question, returning on the downward escalator will allow your vision to fade, leading you back home.

For Your Journal

- Record your opening question or topic.
- Which direction did you go first? Did you opt to go another direction or two following this?
- If you opted not to go a certain direction, what led to that choice? Did you feel you had already acquired enough information the previous direction? Did you feel that the timing was not quite right for exploring it yet? Did you have a sense you needed to avoid it?
- If you went to more than one area, in what order did you explore them? The order you chose may reveal what is easiest versus what is most difficult for you to understand or confront.
- Write about the insights and feedback you received regarding your initial question.
- With the advice you garnered, how might you best carry forward with the addressed situation? What is the next step for you to take?

Post-meditation notes:

Consider this—the directions, either chosen or avoided, may give indication as to what is necessary right now. If you felt reluctance to go a certain direction, it may be indicative of personal unwillingness to view the entire scope of the scenario. Is there a need to open yourself to a new idea or opportunity? Do you have difficulty facing a problem? This is certainly not an absolute. It is possible that the choice is more about the relevance of timing or necessity, but you alone can determine the reasoning. When trying to understand ourselves on a deeper level, the greatest insights tend to arrive by considering all the possibilities.

DOODLE

Before you go into your meditative state, think of a question or topic that is on your mind lately—something for which you would like to receive advice or insight. Jot down your question or topic. Now concentrate on the doodle below. Hold onto this image in your mind as you go into your meditation. For those who are able to keep the meditation going while having your eyes open, this is a perfect opportunity to use that skill now. Ask that pieces of the doodle be used to show you insights into your question. Spend at least five minutes watchfully observing what happens. See what jumps out at you, whether certain sections, colors that form, or shapes. Be open to how the information presents itself to you through this line drawing. When you are done, come back, letting the imagery fade behind you.

For Your Journal

◎ Record your clairvoyant experience, noting how components of the doodle reveal insights to help you answer the question you initially posed.

◎ Using your resources, look up symbolic detail that stands out but does not make immediate sense. Is there a phrase or explanation that completes the information?

◎ How will this newfound knowledge enable you to move forward or proceed with the concern at hand?

◎ More Doodles are available online for free download at www.mandorlaacademy.com/shop

Whenever you want to try the meditation again, you can surely use the same doodle, but you can also make your own 10-Second Doodle to use instead.

To make a 10-Second Doodle, close your eyes and, without hurrying, scribble on your paper at random for ten seconds. Try to vary your drawing motions so intersections of straight and wavy lines will appear.

Why set ten seconds, specifically? Five seconds usually does not allow for an elaborate enough intersecting of lines for the meditation and more than ten seconds tends to result in a bit of writing on unintended surfaces. (In case it is already too late, hairspray is great for removing ink from clothing).

Group Variation:

If you are using this for a group meditation, hand out sheets of blank paper or index cards and let everyone create a 10-Second Doodle, then collect them and have everyone choose out one doodle from the lot for their meditation.

The FOUR DIRECTIONS

To start, think of three topics you would like insight, guidance or wisdom on. These can be of a personal, global, or universal nature. As you are beginning your meditation, do not be surprised if you can smell the lingering scent of pine even before your vision comes completely into focus, because as it does you will find yourself in a clearing encircled by noble pine trees reaching far beyond you. At each of the four cardinal directions of a compass is a single tree, standing within the larger circle.

From where you stand in the center, you can see that every tree has a different color of ribbon tied to a branch. Choosing one of the trees, walk over to it. As you approach, you will see that attached to each ribbon is a paper with a written message related to one of the topics you selected prior to the meditation. Continue to seek out your messages tied to the other trees, until you come to the last one. This tree bears a special message for you from one of your spirit guides.

When you are done collecting your messages, return to the center of the circle, close your eyes, and become conscious of the feelings of peace, warmth, and support that are enveloping you as you arrive home.

For Your Journal

◎   What were your three topics?

○ Record tree by tree, the messages you received and the color of the connecting ribbon.

○ What did you learn through these insights? Write a little about how this will help you. If you had a complex topic in mind that requires more consideration, follow up soon with another insight and guidance meditation to devote time specifically to that one concept.

○ What was your special message from your guide?

○ Go to the *Color Guide* on page 267 to learn more about the significance of the ribbon colors as they pertain to your messages. Add this to your journal entry as well as thoughts you have on your findings.

ALL in GOOD TIME
Cynthia

I went through a building, from a doorway into a dark room and out a pair of French doors. I followed a path up a hill through the woods. The path had wood logs across it on the incline to help walk up without sliding. There was moss along the way. I looked down and saw that I was wearing tan Keds and shorts. When I came to the clearing the sun was shining, but the grass was wet with dew. I lay down in the wet grass and felt the sun on my face and the wet underneath me. Exactly then, an eagle (my totem) circled overhead.

The trees each had a colored ribbon with labels: to my left, red for "pets," in front, green for "career," to my right, blue for "family." On the tree behind me was a yellow ribbon. I gathered the messages, trying to decide whether to stay and read them or to take them home. Choosing to read them there, I sat down in the grass, but I could not make out what they said, so I returned to the building, carrying the messages with me.

Later, I looked at the messages and saw that my guide's message was "Patience."

The message about my pets was, "They are lost sometimes; they feel my loss, but they don't know how to help." *I was not able to see the other two messages yet.*

I found it interesting that when I went back to the circle of trees to read my messages, my eagle swooped down, took the messages out of my hands, and flew off.

RAINBOW STAIRS I

Before you begin, think about a question that you would like guidance on. In a broader sense, you could select an aspect of life or humanity you would like to have more information about instead. That could be on a personal, global, or universal level. As you relax into your meditation, center on this topic. When your vision sharpens, you will be in a dark open space. All you will see is a staircase, faintly illuminated at the base of the lower steps by a red light. Approach the staircase. Know that climbing the stairs will be effortless and invigorating. As you walk up the steps, the light will change through the colors of the rainbow; first from red to orange, then yellow, green, blue, and finally indigo and violet.

Once you reach the top, you will come onto a complete floor lit with bright, energizing, white light. Walk around and familiarize yourself while you are on this level. Look for a window and go over to it. A scene related to the question you asked is shown to you as you look out the window. What you see and hear will be information to provide you with clarity and insight, as to the matter at hand.

When you are finished, turn and you will see a door to exit. Allow everything to fade as you go through the door, again becoming conscious of your breathing, feeling calm and comfortable before you open your eyes.

For Your Journal

◎ Record the question you asked at the beginning of the meditation.

◎ Write down a description of what you saw during your meditation, with extra detail paid to the view from the window.

◎ Include the information you received regarding your question and any direct answer.

◎ Make note of insights that warrant further research. Is there anything you learned that requires you to actively follow up?

The WHITE ROOM
Suzann

I had been to the white room many times by now, a white, straight-backed chair, and me. There was a large picture window on the far side of the room and there was always a hooded figure present, someone about my size. I could not ever see a face, but this person moved as I would expect a woman to move. I often sat in the chair without knowing why. Sometimes I was impatient. Sometimes I was resigned. Sometimes I was disappointed, gave up, and left.

At this point in my life, I was worried sick about my older son: drugs, alcohol, jail, DUI convictions, eviction, and fraudulent checks. It was out-of-control stuff for a 30-year-old man. He kept a job as a cook in a restaurant, but it was not always the same job, or the same restaurant. My son was spiraling down-

ward and I was helpless. Maybe everyone was helpless. How could I live with myself, watching my precious son, whose name means "Gift of the Lord," self-destruct? I needed some perspective, some mental health.

As spring came in Minnesota, I told my son that, in June, he would have to move out for the summer. I needed some space, some time to regroup. He could come back in September when the weather turned cold.

He said, "Where will I go?"

I said, "I don't know. Camp outside, sleep under a bridge; summer won't hurt you."

Three months would be a chance for me to heal a little, but I loved him so much that I would roll up my sleeves and take up the "battle" again in the fall.

That is how we left it—my son, God, me, and the hooded woman who meets me in the white room. We all understood that he would be out by June for three months. No one was looking forward to it, not even me. It was scary, unknown, and risky, but it was without anger, matter-of-fact. It felt like nothingness, actually.

That is what I took to the white room this particular day. With eyes shut, seated on my kitchen chair, I trudged up the many-colored stairs to the white door and entered the room. I sat slumped in the white chair with my head in my hands. I had no energy, not even to breathe. The hooded woman silently came over and stood by me. She put her hand on my arm and knelt beside me, ever so respectfully, ever so gently.

We exchanged no actual words, but I knew she said, "What is it we can do for you?"

Without words, I said, "It's not me. You take such good care of me. But don't you see?" Then I leaned forward in despair. She did see—taking care of me also means taking care of my sons. The woman rose to her feet, her hand still on me to comfort me.

Immediately there was a tapping at that window. It opened and in flew a man, dark-skinned, but otherwise resembling the Mr. Clean character in the old commercials when he hated dirt. He had huge wings, which he folded. He stood with his arms folded, too. I was startled. I had not summoned a scary creature to the white room. Silently I started stammering, "Who is this? What is he doing here? Is he supposed to be here? Only safe things can come here."

They were both ignoring me, this woman who takes good care of me, and "Mr. Clean." They were discussing something without words. It began to dawn on me that he was here in response to her call for help. Help for me. *He received his assignment in a few seconds, whatever it was, turned and leaped out the window into flight.*

It took a few more seconds for me to recover myself. I ran to the window, yelling "Thank you!" several times. He was already winging far away and did not acknowledge me. I sat back down in the chair, still stunned. I was completely sure this powerful creature was on a mission for me, at the request of my guide.

I left the white room that day holding my breath, looking over my shoulder, jumping when the phone rang. Every minute I was expecting news of Mr. Clean beginning his mission. I have never in my life expected God to act as much as the days following that trip to the white room. Ordinary days followed, but I never lost my alertness, as a rabbit, nose twitching, eyes darting, muscles tense, ready to jump, to recognize the work of Mr. Clean. About three weeks passed, and then, there it was.

Mid-May on a Saturday morning, in the middle of my morning devotion and journaling time, my son came upstairs. He was supposed to have gone to work at the restaurant. He moved as if every limb weighed a ton, and his eyes were heavy-lidded.

He had not had time to sleep off whatever high he had produced the night before.

"Are you okay?" I asked, knowing he was not.

"I'm sick," he said. Truer words were never spoken. He always prided himself on going to work, no matter what his condition. Not today. He manned-up enough to call the restaurant. He talked briefly to the manager, one "I'm sorry," and a few seconds later another. Then he said, "I'm sorry you feel that way," and hung up. His part of the conversation was very mature. He looked at me and then, overcome with his ever-present tormentor, Shame, he looked down. "He fired me," was all he said.

I sucked in a desperate breath, and then I froze. This is it. We are on the way. This is Mr. Cleans' first strike. I had been waiting, tensed, but now I relaxed a little. I recognized the beginning of a process here. My poor son was left clueless. Normally, I would have been angry and fierce inside. A job was his last semblance of carrying on, but I was strangely calm. We sat and talked quietly for a few minutes, without judgment, without diminishing a soul. He teared up several times; he really was sorry. Then, because there was nothing left to do, he went back to bed.

I returned to my journal, sitting on the edge of my chair, listening, watching, expecting...what? Would I know it when I saw it?

Certainly not at first, as on Thursday, my son's probation officer called. His message was short and to the point. "Remember your sentence last year? In lieu of jail time, you must complete forty hours of community service and get treatment for drugs and alcohol. What do I have to do to get you to do something? I want to see you next Tuesday. If you have done nothing about this by then, you will go straight to jail."

That was the stroke of midnight. Coaches turn into pumpkins, coachmen back to mice. The reality of now—jail. My son was the solitary person who knew if he was willing to do something, anything, to stay out of jail.

I stayed out of the way. Almost. On Sunday, a friend at church handed me a scrap of paper. It had a first name and a phone number on it. All she said was, "That is the person you call for treatment." I had not asked her. How did she know? I looked over my shoulder, watching for Mr. Clean. The sole sign of him was that scrap of paper.

At home, I handed the paper to my son. It looked very much like something he would lose. I said, "Here is the number you call for treatment. If you call it, good, if you don't, that is up to you."

He called on Monday and set up an appointment. That is what he was able to tell his probation officer on Tuesday. Later he met with the county services person, a gruff, no nonsense guy. (He must really hate dirt). The man explained that treatment would be at Cascade Center as soon as they had an opening, within a few weeks. About payment, it is expensive. What happens if you do not have a job? If you do not have a job, the expenses are taken care of. When my son told me about the meeting, I heard it, saw it, and knew who it was.

By the second week of June, I dropped my son at the recovery center for three weeks of treatment. He did not want to go. It was in-house, and he would be locked in at night. Counseling, telling the truth, discussions with the chaplain, therapy groups, listening. He would be working, working, working, on his spiritual and emotional well-being.

The days passed for him at treatment. His head cleared. To be around him was delightful. At the end of three weeks, we were leaving the center. As we pulled away en route to his next stop, the halfway house, he turned in the passenger seat and gazed at the road behind for a long, last look. "Who'da thought I'd be sad to leave Cascade," he said.

Yeah. Who would have thought?

It was the end of June. He had been out of my house for the first month of summer under the very best care.

My son was as safe as an addict can be at the halfway house. They told him he was doing well, but that he needed to get a job. That very day, he walked across the street to a restaurant he had worked in before and they gave him a job. He was working. Eventually, he completed community service by volunteering at an interfaith program offered through our church. Still at the halfway house, he attracted the attention of girls. True, they were recovering addicts, but it was a new experience for him, one he thought would never happen. He was respected in his group sessions.

His last day at the halfway house was August 28. He had been out of my house for the summer. I was glad to have him back for the winter. Whatever happened, no one could ever take away the wholeness of that summer. To think, it all began in a white room with a window and a straight-backed chair. With my eyes shut, Mr. Clean carried out the Grace of God. With my eyes open, it changed our lives forever.

MORE THAN a DOOR

Select one of the door images on page 88, or from the online printables. For repeating this meditation, consider creating your own set of ten or more door sketches during some free time apart from meditation. Then, when you go to do your meditation, you will have a neat little deck from which to select a card. It is important to note that you should never use photographs of actual doors for this meditation.

The Meditation:
You may enter into this meditation with a question or topic in mind, or you can opt to "see whatever you will" as you journey through it. Hold on to the image or drawing as you begin. Concentrate on the doorway manifesting itself in your meditation. Allow it to appear, taking in the detail as it does. Then, when you are ready, open the door and venture through it. Freely explore the scene you enter. When you have seen all you wanted or needed, then return back through the door and close it behind you. You will be able to return to this very door, or to try other doors in subsequent meditations. The whole process offers unimaginable possibilities.

For Your Journal

◎ Indicate which door you used or tape the drawing into your journal if possible.

○ Describe how the door manifested itself for you as you went into your meditation. Colors? Detailing? Materials? Other aspects of the place surrounding the door?

○ Is this a new place or is it familiar to you?

○ Write about your experience once passing through the doorway. Be sure to include details about the location at which you arrive and describe whether it feels like it is a historic, present, or future environment.

○ If you interacted with anyone in the meditation, be sure to describe the people (names, physical descriptions, etc.), as well as your exchange.

○ Include your final thoughts or impressions. Do you feel there is reason to return to this same place soon? If so, make a note of the time frame of when that should occur if you have a sense of one.

Group Variation:

As a group meditation, it is best to provide each person with two blank index cards. Every participant draws two doors (one on each card). When they are finished, pool all the cards together to make a deck. Take turns blindly selecting a door card until each person has two cards to choose from—one to use now and one to use another time when meditating on their own. It is okay if you end up selecting one of your own drawings, though it is fun to have an extra, unexpected place to visit. Sharing the doorway drawings gets the group more interactively involved, too. Consider having everyone show and compare all the different doors following the meditation. Check out all the different styles, as well as see which doorway sketches turn out remarkably similar. Parallels discovered are a wonderful topic for discussion.

Doorway Meditation Cards

WALL of LIGHT

The starting point of this meditation is apt to vary from one experience to the next, so as your vision clears, be open to the location in which you find yourself. You may see a pastel-colored flowering garden. You may find yourself on a familiar street. You may even be in a scene of your current life. Wherever it is that you find yourself is perfectly fine. Literally or figuratively, the panorama is a represent-tation of your present life. In your scene, bubbles or orbs will appear floating around and above you. There may be several, or one. Follow the orb that catches your eye in a playful, joyful, positive way. The orb will lead you through a shimmering wall, which looks like a curtain of rain, but when you touch it, you discover it is a wall of light. Once you have passed through this curtain of light, you will be shown another place or scene. The message here will be one for your future, either near or more distant. You may even find understanding, resolution, or guidance of the earlier scene where you began your meditation.

Again, follow the orb to return home, as you allow your vision to fade.

For Your Journal

○ What location did you find yourself in at the start of the meditation? If it was somewhere known or familiar to you, was there anything added or altered from its norm or actuality?

○ What significance does this place hold for you, symbolically or literally? What is your clairsentient experience there?

○ Describe the orb or orbs and the wall of light, noting importance as to the effect or colors.

○ Write about the place you discovered beyond the curtain of light.

○ What message did you receive? What are your initial thoughts on the message? Do you feel prompted to follow up with other action? Is there means to resolution based on the insights?

○ How do you feel following the meditation, especially as compared to the opening scene?

Further journaling:

As this meditation relates to your future, spend some time writing about your dreams, goals, and hopes for the future. Consider those things with an open heart to the absolute best possibilities you can imagine—or beyond what you have ever let yourself imagine. Do this without setting expectation or limitations (i.e., no negative self-talk, or justifying away why an experience or outcome could not ever happen). Let yourself visualize these dreams. Create an affirmation for at least one of your aspirations (see page 236).

TURNING OFF FEARS

With knowledge and understanding, fear dissolves.
We must assume more wisdom, for this is
the doorway to our true self, our purpose.

Prior to beginning this meditation, spend a few minutes thinking over the true fears you want to overcome. This does not have to be a chronic phobia. It is more likely to be a hindrance that you have been coping with on a regular basis. Is there a challenge that upsets you, but that is more honestly rooted in fear? Do you have a fear related to your spirituality that is limiting your growth? Decide which fear or fears you would like to address. It is not necessary to take on everything that burdens you at once, as you may easily revisit this meditation periodically.

When you are ready to start meditating, let everything be dark and peaceful. Concentrate on the rhythm of your breathing. The beginning of your meditation will present a house to you. It is possible you will initially be standing inside, but if you find yourself outside, enter the house through the front door. Even if you do not recognize the place, there should be a sense of familiarity and comfort within this building.

Once inside, go to find the door leading to the basement and take the stairs down. There is a small meter room, which is first recognizable from the red light illuminating it. On one wall, you will find a simple dial control that is marked with a range of settings labeled with five levels: off, caution, low, moderate, and high. Take notice of where the level is set at right now. It is possible that there will be more than one dial if you have chosen to address more than one issue, too. Decide what level you are comfortable with setting your fears at for the present. If you feel that you need to use some caution with a certain matter, then turn the dial to that setting. If you feel that a fear is limiting you and is somehow irrational or unfounded, then you may be ready to turn the dial all the way off. As you correct the dials, feel the emerging energy of love and hope that is now available to you. When you are finished making adjustments, you are free to go back upstairs and end your meditation, allowing the house to fade behind you as you leave through the front door.

Upon completing this meditation, you should feel more at peace and be able to focus on genuine endeavors, progressing out of love rather than fear.

For Your Journal

- What fear are you trying to overcome?
- How has it affected your life?
- How do you imagine that conquering this fear will improve your life and free you?
- Describe parts of your meditation that felt especially significant...the house, the meter room, etc.
- How did you find the meter was set when you arrived? Was it set how you would have expected it to be?
- How did you adjust the meter settings?
- Did you notice a change in how you felt from before to after the meditation, either physically or emotionally?

◎ Were you given additional information as to the true
  roots of your fears? How does this help bring you
  resolution and peace?

ECHO MEDITATION

Decide on your questions and topics of concern to start this meditation session. For each question, you will need to pair it with a single verse from a poem, a song lyric, or a phrase from a book. To find the right words, there are three different options. One, turn on some music at random and use the first words you hear. Two, arbitrarily select a book or an insert from a CD case; close your eyes and point at a page, then use that phrase. Three, use a set of prepared song lyric quotes as described in the introduction to the *Lyrical Meditation* on page 170.

No matter how you select your question and phrase pairings, memorize the words so you will be able to repeat them in meditation. When ready, close your eyes and relax into your concentrated meditative state of awareness.

This meditation opens on an idyllic mountainous setting, perhaps the Swiss Alps, the Rockies, Mount Everest in Tibet, or the metaphysically distinguished Mount Shasta.

In meditative state, find a proper vantage point to have echoes occur. As you concentrate on your question, loudly shout out your corresponding phrase. Listen for the echo as it comes back to you, but in the form of a new, resultant message, as opposed to the words you sent out.

You can choose one phrase for each question or topic you have in mind, and then repeat the echo-message process to get all the feedback you need. It is possible to meditate longer for clarity or to ask follow-up questions of your higher self or spirit guides if necessary. If you wish, extend your meditation to travel freely around the area you have found and enjoy the rich beauty and peacefulness for a while before you return.

For Your Journal

◎ Write down your central question, along with the phrase you selected.

◎ Describe the meditation setting. Are you able to identify the place? Do you have a personal connection or synchronicity that immediately comes to mind?

◎ What was your echo reply message? How do you relate or apply this message to your question or situation?

◎ Write down your other questions, phrases, and echo replies, if you covered multiple topics.

◎ Considering the questions you began with, what new things did you learn about the events pertaining to them? How might you utilize the guidance or advice that came through the echo-replies?

◎ If you decided to explore further, make notes about that experience, as you may have happened on a new site of your own to visit in another session.

The TRAIN

As your senses adjust, you will find yourself on the platform of a train station. The passenger train you are about to board is not quite like any other. It is about to take you on a scenic loop, however, the experience you have will vary each time you choose to visit this place in meditation. Most of your journey is dependent upon which of the passenger cars you choose to board.

Walking along the platform, notice that attached to the side of the cars are small signs indicating what sort of information, theme, or guidance you will find while aboard. For example, one says "career," while another reads "family," and yet another says "romance." You will have to read the labels for your own train, so you can choose; they are sure to differ from the examples listed and from person to person or even from session to session.

When you have found a car that looks especially interesting to you on this day, freely board the car and find a seat. The train will depart, travel around the loop, and bring you back to the same platform. During your excursion, be open to all the sights and sounds both within the train car and outside your window.

Should you wish to extend your journey or see the view from another car, please ask the conductor to change your seat. He will hand you a new pass, indicating which car you should try next, and will direct you how to get to it.

When your scenic trip comes to an end, de-board back onto the platform and allow your vision to fade, returning you home.

For Your Journal

○ Describe the train; colors, style of the cars, number of cars, etc. How were they labeled? (Refer to the color and numerology charts if you need to check on symbolism).

○ Which car did you choose to board? What convinced you this was the best place to begin? Was it a visual insight or a feeling you had? Did it correlate to an event going on in your life right now?

○ Were there other people with you? If so, include anything special about this. Do not skip what may have seemed cryptic, especially regarding dialogue, as it may contain a clue or validation you will want to refer back to at some point.

○ What did you see inside the train car?

○ What could you see out your window?

○ What insights did you receive?

○ How do these various pieces relate or bring guidance to you?

○ Did you choose to visit another car? If so, tell about that experience and the insights as well. If there was an exchange between yourself and the conductor, or if how you arrived at the next train car were notable, be sure to write about those details as well. Remember to use your resources to look up significant details that will be beneficial in "translating" your symbolic messages.

CAREER CARS on the TRACK
Heidi

I have used this meditation three times now. I expected to experience and to learn from the places the train went to or from the scenery outside the train, but my personal experience was somewhat different. In all three meditations, I found myself walking along the platform to the head of the train. A friendly conductor came out and escorted me to a car. In the first meditation, the conductor escorted me to a car called "Career." I stepped into the car and it was full of warm, friendly people. There was a table on one side of the car with food and refreshments. The rest of the car was filled with inviting, bench-style, upholstered seats. I felt welcomed and comfortable. I am not sure that I was even aware of where we went on the train. The feeling was one of great rapport with the people I was with, and a relaxed atmosphere. This was meaningful to me in that I have been using an affirmation regarding a new job that I would like to have come my way. In this job, I am able to utilize the best of my skills as part of a wonderfully supportive group of people doing meaningful work. This train car had an air of that. In addition, the presence of a table was significant in that the table to me is a symbol of a place to gather, work, talk, and share, in both home life and work life, so I was pleased to see it there.

The second time I did the meditation, the conductor escorted me to a very beautiful, midnight blue car with images of waves and seashells on the outside. There was no name on the car, but I knew exactly what the outside of the car symbolized to me. As I stepped inside, I was enveloped in ease and calm. There was a silk-lined, midnight blue nest/bed that I crawled into, with a downy pillow on which I lay my head. The train started up and the motion of the train car was soothing. This meditation was all about nurturing and nourishment. Although it felt like I would fall asleep, I did not, and it was a nice, ten-minute deep relaxation.

To explain why this second meditation was symbolic for me, I often meditate visualizing a path. This path takes me to the ocean, where I dive into the waves. I swim deeper and deeper until I come to "my place." Here I meet my ocean mother and my spirit guide father. Sometimes I get interesting information, but often I plainly get the centered rejuvenation of connecting to "the deep" or the unconscious. Sometimes it takes a long while to get to that place. Some days I am unable to. It is hard to describe, but I have to be in the right place of ceding control (not forcing the image) and being alert (not letting go so much that I fall asleep). When I saw the "ocean car," I had to laugh a little— "the deep" had transformed to a train car.

In my third time doing the train meditation, I walked down the platform as before, but this time the conductor met me with some clothes he carried. He said, "You may wish to change into these." He then took me to a car labeled, "Total Future." A debonair gentleman met me at the door to the car and escorted me inside. I was already, magically, in my attractive, slim dress suit. We sat together in our car; eventually we reached the destination. Leaving the train, we went into a boardroom, joining a lovely, sophisticated group of individuals around a table. Again, the table is symbolic of an ideal collaboration to me, in this case, in a more formal setting. The room was pretty much made up of windows, lots of light. The colors were light or white. I do not recall conversation. Rather than the formality making this experience less genuine than that of my fun, relaxed "career car," the setting and formality suggested to me a meeting at a higher, more evolved level, still utterly genuine and present. We then re-boarded the train and returned.

I am thinking a lot about my career and life purpose right now, finishing a college degree and becoming certified as a holistic coach. Smack dab in my midlife, working to discover and uncover the next section of my path. I think these meditations gave some generalized information that became even clearer as I wrote them down.

ST. VALENTINE MEDITATION:
For Honoring or Attracting a Love

Valentine's Day. To some, the perfect opportunity to break out their big fat markers, construction paper, and frilly paper doilies in the spirit of a creative romantic, revisiting their long ago primary school days. To others, it is one of those regrettable days, requiring swift action to produce a token of their affections for their loved ones, who have indubitably been planning for the holiday for some 364 days. To others still, a painful occasion to endure yet another rant on the commercialization of romance by someone who clearly has a significant other and thereby, no concern about another's lack thereof. Irrespective of your personal circumstance or your viewpoint on how black or rosy the day of St. Valentine may be—here is a Valentine to you, from me.

The Meditation:
Take a few minutes to yourself to be somewhere quiet, play some soft music, light some candles, whatever you want to do to create a nice atmosphere for your meditation. Get comfortable wherever you would like to sit or lie down. Close your eyes. Let everything be dark and still. Center your thoughts on your breathing and surround yourself in this peacefulness. When you are ready, allow your meditative senses to get going. You will find yourself outdoors. Absorb your surroundings, the sights, sounds, and smells of the nature around you. There is a path of some type—walking trail, sidewalk, cobblestone lane—for

you to meander along, follow this until you come to point where it divides into two directions.

The trail to the left is for those who wish to honor a relationship you are in currently.

The trail to the right is for those who wish to discover a *new* relationship.

Those taking the route to the left will arrive at a spacious, open area where you will find two trees standing side by side. In the lower branches of these trees are colorful lengths of satin cord. Choose a color you find appealing, tying it around the trunks of the two trees so the cord joins them. Take a moment to sit beneath the trees and as you do, think of three qualities that you most appreciate about your significant other, also think of three things you most want to offer to the relationship as you move forward from this day. As you come up with these ideas, say, or think to yourself, "I am grateful for your presence in my life and honor you as we grow from here."

If you take the route going to the right, you will come to a spacious, open area where you will find one tree there already growing, and one yet to plant. Plant this tree next to the first, using the water source you find to feed it. You will see that the water has more of a magical quality to it, colorful and radiant like light. Somewhere in or near the first tree, search for a piece of rose quartz. Once you have it, take this pink stone and place it on the ground directly between the two trees, thinking of the three most important things that you wish to offer into a new relationship. As you kneel or sit there, think or say to yourself, "I am opening my heart to you and have grown to a place within myself that I am now ready for you to be a part of my life."

From whichever clearing you are at, see yourself surrounded in shimmering, warm, white, pink, and green light, feeling how positive, peaceful, and healing it is. Walk back down the path that you came from and allow your vision to fade as you once again become aware of your breathing before you open your eyes.

For Your Journal

◎ What were your initial impressions of your surroundings...the type of landscape, sounds, smells, etc.?

◎ Did you choose the path to the left? If so, what color of cord did you select? What does that mean to you, and what is the traditional symbolism?

◎ For the path to the left—do you know what kind of trees you joined? Were they of the same or different species? Are there symbolic ways in which these two trees represent you and your loved one? (*Symbolism of Flowers & Trees*, page 277).

◎ For the path to the left—what three ideas did you decide you would like to bring to the relationship and why?

◎ For the path to the right—if the already planted tree is a representation of you, what does the kind of tree, or its appearance, mean to you?

◎ For the path to the right—what kind of tree do you plant in representation of the loved one you wish to welcome into your life? What qualities of this tree are symbolic of the person?

◎ For the path to the right—what three aspects do you most want to offer to a new relationship? Are the aspects ones you would have anticipated previously, or were they decided upon having gained new awareness?

◎ For either path—add further details about the meditation you experienced, including your feelings comparing before you began the meditation to how you felt at the end of your session.

◎ Journal new insights as they come to light over the next few weeks regarding yourself and relationships.

◎ Consider that time following the meditation might be a perfect chance for penning that special love letter or a Valentine love poem for your beloved. Even if they are not yet with you, it will keep.

BONFIRE MEDITATION

Think of a personal fault, futile life aspect, or a fear that you would like to purge or free yourself from before you begin this meditation. Once you have settled on one idea, mentally assign it an object to give it a tangible symbol; you will "carry" this object with you into your meditation. To help set the intention for your meditation, it is a good idea to write this down in your journal.

As you start, entering meditative state brings you to a place where there is a gathering already assembling. All are kindly welcome here. Aside from bringing along symbolic objects, everyone present has brought something to share...berries, nuts, cider, pumpkin bread, and more. Share all the treats in the circle. (It is a fine opportunity to practice your clairgustance). This begins the casual ceremony of healing and renewal.

At the appropriate time, throw the old thing—your symbolic object—into the fire. Others will be participating in the activity there as well. Once everyone has done this, you all pass around a wooden box. Each person puts one small token of his or her own into this box. This token item is positive or meaningful to the person, but it is also deemed ready to move on to someone new. The box is handed around the circle one time for adding items to it; the box is passed around the circle a second time, so that every person chooses out one new article to take home. This new token will fill the space left empty by the fire offering. You can take it home with you and allow it to be a message of hope. When you are reminded of your token at some point in the future, consider it a sign to return to do the meditation again; you can exchange it then, as someone else may be in need of it, just as you may be in need of a new item yourself.

For Your Journal

○ What is the symbolic item you decide on at the start of your meditation? What does it represent to you? Is there a predicament going on that brings you to draw upon that aspect and choose that item right now?

○ Describe the healing ceremony, the environment, and the people in attendance as you go in to join them in this celebration.

○ Include a few words about the shared treats and your ultra-sensory taste experience.

○ Write about ridding yourself of the unwanted item, and about the token you place in the box, as well as the token you choose to bring home with you. Include details and information about the symbolism of this new token, and how receiving it makes you feel.

○ Record other notable happenings connected with this meditation or synchronicities in the few days following your meditation session.

LETTING GO
Coralee

I brought a giant purple sweater to the bonfire. I think it may represent hanging on to my "fat clothes," because I cannot really believe and trust that the weight I worked so hard to lose will not come back. Plus, there is the way I hang onto my past through my wardrobe.

When the box came around, I put in a roll of duct tape. It feels like maybe I have to let go of always trying to fix things and let them be the way they are sometimes.

When the box came back around, it was much bigger than before, and I took out a French horn. I used to play it in junior high. I don't think the message was about taking it up again, but maybe some more general type of musical skill I have left dormant.

LIFE'S DOORWAYS

You will see a bright, lovely corridor with several rooms along one side of it when your vision becomes clear. Curtains or doors are at each entryway, some of which will be open, while others are closed.

By being observant to which open room you feel most drawn to, choose the one you want to enter. Within this room, you witness a scene from your life. It may be present day or in your past, but either way, it is a moment that is still strongly influencing you. While here, you can learn how this situation is truly affecting you and why it is important for you to move beyond this. Stay as long as you wish in your chosen room and take your time to discover the information you need to have in order to make the choice of how to proceed when you leave the room. Do you wish to move past this and are you ready to close the door on the specific matter?

Within the room, you will receive helpful guidance. You will be able to ask questions so that your understanding of the event satisfies you. Importantly, too, you will be able to ask for or see which new doors along the corridor open to you as a result of the one door closing. Knowing this helps you make the decision about whether or not to close the door on the first room.

When you are ready, exit the room either closing the door behind you or leaving it open, as you have decided. Do not feel forced to make sudden changes if you feel you need more time to think about it. It is always an option to come back during another meditation session to close the door, but you will at least now have the awareness and wisdom needed to guide you until the time you are ready for closure.

For Your Journal

○ Describe the corridor and give detail to anything that was especially significant to you.
○ Write down the reasoning behind choosing the room you first enter. Is it something about the look or feel of it? Is it because you have a sense of need or urgency to investigate it?
○ Explain what transpires in the room.
○ What are your thoughts about closing or leaving open this door and how do you arrive at your decision?
○ Do not forget to record the questions you asked and all the guidance you received through this experience. Especially if you have left the door open, anticipate receiving advice you need prior to doing another session intended for closure.

Further journaling:

Take some time to reflect on how you typically handle events from your past. Do you tend to hold on to aspects or issues that are no longer useful or constructive factors in your present? Have you moved past important events with indifference or avoidance? Think about how your usual way of reacting to challenges works well or poorly for you. Even if a past situation was terrible, are you able to think of one bi-product from the experience that was good or positive; maybe even a remotely related effect that came about years later? That one thing, in spite of significance, may be enough to recognize a flicker of good. It may be sufficient to find gratitude for that alone, allowing you to be fully untethered from the rest. Use an affirmation to help create this new freedom for your future. (See page 236 for *How to Write an Affirmation*).

LABYRINTH

The wording for this activity meditation enables readers to use the labyrinth illustration (page 114 or full-color online printable), however, if you are lucky enough to have access to a public labyrinth nearby, modify the meditation to use while actually walking through it.

Aside from reflection and relaxation, labyrinths can be used with intention of communicating with your higher self, spirit guides, or the Universe. Labyrinths work in two different ways when using them for gaining insights. The first method is carrying out a heightened, constant communication. You begin with one question, focusing on that as you enter the labyrinth and quickly receive your answer. This allows for a continual question-answer conversation. Approaching the labyrinth in this way works best if you have short questions or a series of them for inquiry. An example would be asking a string of yes/no questions, perhaps building up to a main question asked at the center.

The second way is to focus on a complex question or topic as you enter the labyrinth, with the intention to receive detailed information about the matter. With this method, concentrate on the question and topic as you enter, mulling over various details, memories, or events that give rise to your question. The basic idea here is that until you reach the center of the labyrinth, you are the one doing the "talking." The return path is the opportunity for listening and receiving guidance.

Some believe that energy and awareness escalate as you walk further into the pattern, with the crest at the center, and then diminishing as you exit. From my experience, this is entirely dependent upon the individual and the particular labyrinth. For some it is like that, a gradual elevation. For others, stepping one foot into a labyrinth is like flipping a light switch. It is a good to reminder, however, to pay attention to your personal energy and to how it shifts. That way you can plan and personally adapt the style of your meditation around energy levels to get the most benefit.

The Meditation:

Before beginning this reflection meditation, think of a question you would like insights on, considering which of the aforementioned ways you would like to pursue the experience. Now imagine how this labyrinth design on paper looks to you in your meditation; let it come to life. Next, visualize an object that you would like to leave as a gift of thanks. A flower, a shell, a pretty stone, or a cup of wine...it is entirely up to you. Once you have this gift manifested in your mind, you are ready to enter the labyrinth. "Walk" through the labyrinth illustration by tracing your finger along the trail shown in the picture in a conscious, relaxed state of mind until you arrive at the center, at which point you can then close your eyes and allow yourself to fall completely into the imagery.

If you are at an actual labyrinth, walk through the entire course completely in a light meditative state with your eyes open. The gift you bring may be an actual little token to express your gratitude.

Spend as much time in contemplation as you would like at the center of the labyrinth. Be still, open, and calm. Allow your ultra-senses to carry insights to you, as you listen, watch, and feel. Know that the information you need will come.

When you are ready to leave, place your gift on the larger stone at the labyrinth's center. Depart the maze reversing the route you used to enter, allowing feelings of peace, gratitude, and joy to envelope you. Quietly listen for messages as you meander back.

For Your Journal

○ Record the date and type of labyrinth you used.
○ Which method for walking the labyrinth did you try? How did it work for you? What might you change for next time?
○ What was the gift you brought into the labyrinth? Did it have special meaning to you?
○ What was the question you set intention to have answered?
○ How did you feel as you were entering the maze?
○ Describe your experience concerning energy levels (yours, and that of the labyrinth). Were there fluctuations that you noticed?
○ What were your feelings as you returned out of the labyrinth?
○ Of course, record any messages that were received.

Classic Labyrinth

HEALING LIGHT

If an aura is the natural energy field that surrounds each of us, our *chakras* then are the points within our auras, which allow this energy to flow. This distributes our life force energy throughout our bodies. Working with our chakras, by means of visualization and meditation, helps us to heal, restores and balances our energy, and rids us of unwanted energy.

Before beginning, take a minute to familiarize yourself with the seven primary chakras we will consider for the purpose of this meditation, as shown in the illustration. Beginning with the first chakra, red, at the base of the spine, going upward to orange at the abdomen, yellow at the solar plexus, green at the heart, blue at the throat, indigo at the forehead, and ending with the seventh chakra, purple, at the crown of the head.

These last two I have mentioned are fairly close in proximity, so some people perceive purple at the forehead and white at the crown chakra bypassing the indigo; while those that do distinguish between indigo and purple, typically see a separate eighth chakra located slightly above their heads that is white. However this appears, it is fine.

When it comes to the heart chakra, some people see pink rather than green, or even a spiraling blend of green and pink. If you experience one of those possibilities personally, it is not out of the norm. It is all purely a matter of perception. Remember to think of the chakras as multi-dimensional energy — it is not merely a flat disc at the front or center of the body.

Primary Chakras

The Meditation:

As your meditative awareness moves away from your breathing toward imagery, you will find yourself walking along a sandy beach. Notice your surroundings. You will see someone walking far ahead of you in the distance. If you watch closely, that person places an object in the sand and walks away. From where you are at, you can tell that it is metallic, as its mirror-like surface sparkles with the reflection of the sun. As you reach the object, kneel down to look at it and you will discover that it is a metallic glass sphere, quite similar to those people display in their gardens. It has been left here for you, so bring it with you to a place where you feel comfortable sitting. Hold the sphere on your lap or set it in front of you while you do the following energy cleansing exercise.

The opening and closing of our chakras is a process we do as a visualization to manage our chakras and energy. This allows us to cleanse our own energy purposefully. It can increase our awareness, rejuvenate us, and heal us.

Imagine opening one chakra at a time, working from the bottom and going upwards. Visualize freely each chakra, whether as a flower, a sphere, or a different way that you perceive it. Once you open a chakra, cleanse, and repair it by showering it with a pure, brilliant sparkling light of the corresponding color. Watch each chakra become renewed and restored by this light of God (again, by whatever name you recognize your Divine presence), and of the Universe. When you are finished, close the chakras and lock them up tight, working in reverse order, top to bottom.

Now, crack open that metallic glass sphere. Be surrounded in the released, brilliant light. This light is a gift from your healing guide, who you saw in the distance earlier, placing the sphere in the sand for you. After you have fully experienced this healing light, close your eyes and bring your awareness back home.

For Your Journal

◎ What color is the metallic sphere that you find?
◎ Describe special facets of the beach setting of this meditation and include all the sensory components of this experience.
◎ How did you perceive your chakras? (Particularly notate this regarding the purple/indigo/white positions and the green/pink of the heart).
◎ What color of healing light did the sphere emit? Write your understanding of how it is intended to help you (generally or specifically).
◎ To see if additional meanings stand out, corresponding to the color of your sphere, refer to the *Color Guide* on page 267.

COLORS OF HEALING
Carol O.
Remarks on a variation of the *Healing Light* meditation

The first color that came to me was red. I knew that I was supposed to look at my root chakra. When I opened the chakra, I noticed something that looked like black vines coming from inside. As I pulled on the vines to remove them, I went further inside my body. The vines were clinging to my intestines, strangling them. I removed them, all the way down to the roots and disintegrated them into white light.

Next, I saw the color orange. With that abdomen chakra, there were also vines strangling the intestines. I removed those also.

Then, the color yellow came up. My solar plexus chakra had no vines. I looked inside of my body and saw my inflamed organs, surrounded by an angry red color. I sent healing light inside to calm my organs. Tulku, my totem guide, in a human form, was also there sending healing light, stroking the organs like you would pet a cat. The organs lost their red color and decreased in size.

That was the last color that I saw. The relevance of the meditation was that at the time, I was hospitalized due to a severe illness that had presented itself through gastrointestinal symptoms, excessive weight loss, and dehydration.

🌿 Unwanted Energy & Hugging the Earth

Every moment of every day, outside energy (energy that is not of our own body's system) influences us. From our interactions with others to the environments we navigate, everything we do is an association of energies. The constructive energy, that which heals and balances us is often easier to accept, however, there is the opposite force of energy that is overwhelming, burdening, or harmful. What should a person do about unwanted, excess, or "negative" energy?

I do not like to refer to energy as negative or positive when avoidable, because it is relative (even before a lapse into conversation over the science of energy). What is comfortable or necessary to one person is not the same to another. What is vital or acceptable to you one day, may not be the next, so to say *unwanted* energy is fitting.

Sometimes in meditation, you will work with energy for your own healing purposes. While you could ignore the energy influencing your system that feels bad, unneeded, murky, dulling, or like it is holding you back in some way, usually you do not want to leave it how it is—it will not feel right otherwise—and you want to alter it somehow. A practical way to deal with it is to visualize removing that unwanted energy, sending it away from you with the best intentions that it will go back to where it came from, or that it positively applies in some other place. Think of it as fertilizer: causing a big stink upfront, but when put to good use, highly beneficial to its purpose. Imagine the energy moving away from you in any number of ways—wildly zooming away, exploding into a billion sparkling particles of brilliant light, or seeing it as tiny pink and green hearts flying away. Despite the method, intend that all the energy go out into the Universe with nothing but love, joy, and good thoughts.

If you feel like you want to do something more concrete than that, you can always try ground hugging or tree hugging. It is entirely as it sounds. Literally, hug the tree you choose or lie on the ground with your arms spread wide and give the Earth a squeeze. As you do either, imagine that excess or unwanted energy, bad feelings, stress, or anxiety, drains away from you, soaked up by the Earth or the tree. That outpouring of energy transmutes immediately into a force, which is useful and healing to the world.

CYCLES

If you find yourself at a point in life where it feels like the same situations keep repeating themselves, it can be a very stressful and confusing part of the spiritual journey. At times, cycles are about issues that recur, but they may also pertain to other life aspects. For example, a cycle may involve the same kinds of people who keep entering your life, or relationships that are all too similar. A very common cycle is worry. People tend to worry about a specific life aspect, unsure of how to break the pattern, even when they discover there was nothing to worry about and all too soon, the cycle repeats and the worry starts all over again.

To make a new start or to break the cycle in one's life, it is necessary to start acting or re-acting in different ways than in the previous instance. The good news is that even the smallest change to our patterns and habits has tremendous transformational influence. Deciding what alteration to test out can be challenging to do if you do not even comprehend what the cycle is, what other life aspects are connected, or what is influencing the cycle in the first place.

The following meditation will assist you in understanding the cycle and interconnecting aspects, which in turn will allow you to either enhance or break the cycle.

The Meditation:

When you are relaxed and ready to begin, let your ultra-senses attune to find yourself in an old blacksmith shop. On one of the workbenches, you will find a coil of chain spiraled neatly. There are many links. Inspect the chain and the individual links in whatever way you are inclined. Are they all the same? Do any appear different in size, shape, or due to distinguishing marks? These links represent various aspects of your life, including the people and the cycles intended for you to understand. For those you are wishing to learn more about, ask questions about them. What do they represent? Whom do they represent? Do they feel or look like a positive or a negative influence?

Once you have gained enough information, use a chain cutter to remove those links you want to disconnect from, thereby allowing you to heal or move forward from your present circumstance. Polish up links you thoughtfully feel drawn to keep. Life being as complex as it is, perhaps you are aware of links you truly need to remove, but you are not yet prepared to do so. This is fine. You still will have a greater understanding of your concerns by being unconditionally open to the knowledge gained here. At any time in the future, you can certainly come back to your chain coil in meditation, so you can alter it accordingly.

When you are satisfied with the chain, make sure you have reconnected breaks you have made, then coil the chain back on the workbench. Allow the shop to fade behind you as you leave to return home.

For Your Journal

◎ Write your description of the blacksmith shop and of the coiled chain that you find there.
◎ Explain how you chose to work with the chain and the individual links.

- Are there links that you leave alone to work on during a future session? What do they represent?
- What is your feeling, emotional or mental state, as you are entering the shop? How does this change or differ as you conclude your meditation?
- What awareness of your personal cycles or life themes emerged?
- What is the smallest change you think you could make to attempt to alter or break that cycle? In actuality, even the tiniest change in our behavior patterns, habits, and routines can be enough to completely alter a cycle and bring new opportunities for other steps to a goal. Sometimes all it means is relaxing and giving Divine timing an extra day to work it out.

TRAVEL

This meditation is for the purpose of exploring and gaining new insights and information.

Before you read ahead, first choose two numbers between 1500 and 2500 and write them down.

Finished?

Next, choose two more numbers from one through twelve and record one below the first number you wrote down and the other below the second number, like this:

1732	2057
2	8

After you have done this, you can begin your meditation ritual. At the start of this journey, you will be in a wide-open outdoor area, such as a field, a vacant parking lot, or the desert. As you walk out toward the center of this place, you will find a futuristic-looking chamber. You have discovered your personal time machine. Enter the chamber and input the first pairing of numbers (which is your chosen year and month) with the intention then set for the machine to transport you to a place of significance at that point in time.

Once there, investigate outside the vessel to learn what is important for you to see and know about. Be open to the scenes, cultures, events, or locations presented to you without presupposition or expectation. Return to the chamber when you are ready to input the second pairing of numbers. Spend as much time as you would like to search in and around your second destination as well.

When you would like to return, use the control panel to input the month and year for today. As you walk home back across the open space you started out in, consider significant messages or relationship between the two dates. What have you learned that gives insight into your present situations?

Note: This meditation is an intended method for gaining an understanding of how history and future can provide deeper awareness of our present (personally or globally). However, it still is possible that an actual past life memory or familiar events can resurface through this exercise, too. If this does happen, keep yourself separated from the scene, taking a position as a mere witness to the account, knowing there is a positive reason for you to see or reconnect to this information. Then, when you are done, record the experience in detail as usual. If its purpose is not immediately clear, review what you have written in your journal again in a couple of days with a freely objective perspective to see what importance, parallels, or details resonate with your present life.

For Your Journal

◎ Record your selected numbers.
◎ Describe your personal time machine and the area where you located it.
◎ Detail the experiences you have in both destinations. What aspects most drew your attention? Did you hear or read anything while you were there?

- What, if any, are the parallels between the two dates? Is there an overall theme and if so, does it relate to events in the present time you are aware of, whether on a personal or global level?
- How does the acquired information shed light onto present life matters for you? What may be the direct and indirect messages of this experience?
- When you revisit this meditation and your time machine, consider using it to navigate even more possibilities. Try selecting a time you have always been curious about...whether that is a time of a historic event, or a time you believe you lived another life. Alternatively, you could choose a time in the future you that would like to peek at. This is a fun and safe way to explore what we could otherwise not.

TREE of LIFE:
Meditation for the New Year or a Spring Celebration

Walk ahead in your meditation across an expansive lawn or field. There stands a lone tree with an assortment of colorful ribbons streaming down from it. Each ribbon attaches to a small gift or box. Decide whether to pull down either three or four; then select the ones you want to collect according to which ribbon colors you are attracted to in the moment. The order and the ribbon colors will have significance, so thoughtfully keep track as you go.

Once you have them all, open your gifts in the same order that you chose them. Find out if there is anything special to know about each item. Take time to ask questions or to invite related insights to emerge. When you return, take the same path leading away, letting the scene fade behind you.

Following your meditation, refer to the *Gift and Ribbon Color Key* on page 130 to find out more information about the gifts and the intended meaning behind the ribbon colors. Look up the kind of tree to see if additional symbolism applies (*Symbolism of Flowers & Trees*, page 277).

For Your Journal

○ Describe the scene of your meditation. Is there significance to the season of the setting? (Does it appear the same as what it is to you presently?)

- List the ribbon colors and gifts received in sequence. Highlight this list with additional information you received about the gifts.
- Refer to the key on page 130 and make note of each gift's purpose and the associated ribbon colors. Journal about synchronicity regarding the information or understandings you have initially.
- At a later date, refer back to your notes to add updates and validating stories to your experience.

BOLD BEGINNING
Jami

Regarding a variation on the *Tree of Life* meditation

The meditation we did asked that we leave something behind as we move forward into the New Year. I walked across a windswept hillside up to my tree. It was very blustery. The wind swirled around the tree trunk, up, around and through the branches. The something I left behind for the past year was my self-doubt in the shape of a dirty rock. Given to me via my search through the branches was a golden apple representing knowledge, so that I may teach others. The apple looked like I could lift the lid off. Inside was a shiny white tooth — Truth. It was a play on words — I laughed! I am to be bold and audacious, "like your President Obama." I kicked the rock to the side and carried the golden apple away.

Gift & Ribbon Color Key

Gift Meanings:

Gift #1　　This is a gift from your guides to celebrate the New Year (or spring season) and/or something to help you for the coming months.

Gift #2　　This item is a symbol or key to your path for the next six months, approximately.

Gift #3　　This gift represents a message about love, family, or friendship.

Gift #4　　The fourth gift, if you chose to select this optional one, is a message regarding a "mission" for you in upcoming months. It is a message about learning, work or career, personal or spiritual growth, or health.

Ribbon Color Significance:

Pink	gentleness	Blue	empathy
Red	passion	Dark Blue	safety
Orange	change	Green	hope
White	forgiveness	Purple	wisdom
Yellow	joy	Violet	nostalgia
Gold	bounty	Black	listening
Gray	protection	Silver	grace
Peach	responsibility/caring		

WEEK or MONTH AHEAD

The idea for this activity meditation came to me when I was considering my options for creating a prediction-based meditation. It was some years after a conversation with a student about how he perceives insights about personal future events. I recalled the experiences he had described and discovered this translates really well into a meditation that everyone can use.

In your journal or on a separate piece of paper, sketch out a calendar for a week, month, or number of days toward which you are interested in looking ahead. Sometimes working out a calendar from tomorrow until the end of the month you are currently in is a good option, too. The future is not fixed or pre-determined, so it is not recommended to undertake more than a month. If you hold open your journal in front of you while you meditate, you can quickly transfer notes from your meditation to your written copy as soon as you are done.

Take the calendar you have prepared with you mentally as you go into your meditation. To see how these days may progress for you, watch intently, as days appear to be highlighted, or light up. Colors are coded green for positive, yellow for more neutral, or red for caution or awareness. It is quite possible to see your own personal color-coding. You can set intention to change the above colors, or wait to see if you naturally perceive a variation and ask then what the shade represents.

If you wish, ask questions or ask for details on any of the dates. The information you receive will be dependent upon how much you are *allowed* to know in advance. You may get complete scenes or details, you may get small clues, or you may not get anything at all some days. Completely be accepting of what you are taking in and make note of it when you return. It is all meant to help raise awareness.

We have free will to make our own choices and therefore, sometimes, to modify outcomes, so consider that events may be altered on the calendar based on what you opt to do with the knowledge you receive. Looking ahead means that in the very moment you do it, the insights you see are based on that precise moment. A red *caution* date is not a permanent marker of doom; it is a message to "Be aware; be watchful." Use it as a notice to be prepared or to shift perspective so you are not caught off-guard, then it can help you choose how you approach or handle a problem. A little preparation helps us navigate ways to bring our best selves to those days ahead.

For Your Journal

- Note the colors and their indications and mark these on your journaled calendar.
- Record insights, words, clues, or even feelings that arose as you were concentrating on certain days. Sometimes a minute detail brings the greatest validation later on.
- During and after the phase of time your calendar depicts, be sure to make note of all that is significant, accurate, or possibly changed by having a perspective of advance awareness.

◎ Come back to the calendar later to add remarks on how the activity helped, including differences of outlook, attitude, awareness, patience, and positivity.

◎ Be mindful of which approaches work the best for you. If you have truer results from one session to the next, you will be able to adapt the meditation be more reliable for yourself.

ASPECTS of LIFE:
Year-Ahead Insights

You can try this meditation at any point during the year, but the aim is to receive insights, news, or signs for the period of a full year ahead.

To prepare for your meditation, you will need to write these following eight words or phrases on separate scraps of paper: career, health, intellectual/personal growth, family, finances, friendships, love relationships, spiritual growth. These are eight main facets of life. Fold the paper pieces so you cannot tell which phrases are on them. Mix them up and set them aside. On a separate piece of paper or a journal page, write a vertical list of numbers, one through eight.

Open yourself meditatively to your ultra-sensory awareness, setting the intention to gain needed insights regarding those eight aspects of your life. As soon as you feel connected, write down a list of adjectives, one next to each number. It does not matter if you arrive at the list by particular means. Use the first words that come to mind, like filling in blanks for *Mad Libs*. If not that, you could select a book and randomly flip through pages to select adjectives. Either way, try to relax and trust that the right descriptive words will come to you.

Once you have your word list, open one of the folded papers. Write that life aspect next to your first listed adjective, open the second, and write that next to your second adjective on the list and so forth, until you have recorded all eight of the life aspects.

At this point, you can go into your meditation. Allow the setting and environment to reveal itself. Once settled there, you will be able to open eight individual boxes containing small items or clues to future events, doing this will enhance and elaborate on details and messages regarding the individual life aspects that you receive. Use remaining time to clarify symbolism and ask pertinent questions. Finish the meditation by asking either for the theme of the year, or for a synopsis message.

For Your Journal

○ Be sure to record all eight of the life aspects and the corresponding adjectives, adding the details and messages as you receive them throughout opening the boxes.
○ Write down impressions that are potentially premonitory, as well as other signs to watch for over the coming months.
○ Which of the eight aspects looks as though it may be the most challenging, time consuming, or rewarding?
○ Which ones are the most exciting, hopeful, or mysterious?
○ Which ones have the most clarity or confusion surrounding them?
○ What is the theme for the year? If you receive a concluding message, be sure to write it down. These ideas may be useful in creating an affirmation to use throughout the year.

NEW YEAR'S INSIGHT

The purpose behind this meditation is to gain insights and guidance for a new year beginning, but it could work as easily focusing on a three, six, or nine-month period instead. With that in mind, predetermine the amount of time that you wish to study before you begin.

Imagine yourself at a vast area. Possibilities include a city, a zoo, a shopping mall, or a national park. You are free to explore the different areas to people-watch, or to find a quiet place there to absorb the tranquility. However you begin, use these first moments to relax and enhance your meditative state.

When you are ready to move ahead, be aware of the following three features within the area. The first site is a scenic overlook. Use the viewing glasses provided there. Looking through the glasses presents insight as to what you can look forward to in the new year.

Moving through the park once again, find the vending cart. This is your second stop. The items sold here reveal information as to your path or purpose for the coming months.

The direction signs along the walk supply your third source for insight. These signs are indicative of what you need to be prepared for in advance. They provide clues as to what to be aware of moving forward into this stage of your life journey.

Once you have acquired the information you need, walk away from your location allowing the place to fade into a swirl of colors behind you as you return.

For Your Journal

- ⊙ In the opening moments of the meditation used for relaxing, what did you most notice about the park setting?
- ⊙ Describe all that you saw through the viewing glasses at the scenic overlook. Based on what you saw, write a summary sentence; include what you will be looking forward to in the new year. Perhaps you can write an affirmation to support this, too. (page 236)
- ⊙ What items sell from the vending cart? What does this signify to you? How does this give light to your life path or purpose for the coming months?
- ⊙ What did the direction signs read? Is there a cumulative message? Do you need to take action or is it about having advanced awareness toward events or issues?
- ⊙ During your walk, were you significantly drawn to anything unusual or remarkable? Did you witness other happenings in the park? How do you interpret this?
- ⊙ What were your initial feelings and emotions coming out of the meditation?
- ⊙ Did you get an impression of a personal theme for the designated time?

Further journaling:

Actively create your year using the following outline as a template. Complete the sentences by writing your intentions for the best possible scenarios in the months ahead. Even if you do not know how these ideals might manifest themselves, detail your dreams as though this is happening right now. Write sentences in the present tense describing your desired situations and elaborating as much as possible.

20_____ is the best year yet!

I feel fulfilled because:

I achieve my goals:

My relationships (love, family, friendships) are:

My (job/work/school) is rewarding:

I am healthy and happy:

I am pleased with my financial standing:

In my personal life I am:

My spiritual life is:

YOUR HIGHER SELF

When you begin, you will find yourself in a tranquil park, similar to those of the early 1900's, when people would go for afternoon strolls along the pathways and boardwalks, among the trees and aromatic flower gardens. Find the trail that wraps around the small lake. If you see other people as you are walking, continue until you find a private place to sit where you will be able to enjoy the view and peacefulness. Whether you choose to sit on a quiet bench, or on a blanket on the lawn, or under a tree, find whatever place suits you. Take in your surroundings, relax, and absorb the scenery. Reflect on whatever stands out. Later, you can research symbolic messages received to find their meanings.

Watch for a figure approaching in the distance and invite the person to join you. Be open to the energy and allow yourself to connect to this being of light, your higher self. Have a conversation, using this opportunity to express your concerns and frustrations, then listen and allow your higher self a chance to respond, giving advice, and support. Include questions to ask your higher self such as, "Is there anything I should be aware of now?" or "Are there messages I need to hear?"

When you are done, you can close your eyes as you sit there, taking time to think through the messages and answers you have received before opening your eyes, returning home.

For Your Journal

- What is your park like? Aside from describing it, sketch a little map of the park, including important aspects you notice there.
- Which finer details stood out to you most? Use your resources to decipher symbolic messages.
- Write a description of your higher self. What are the similarities and differences to your present-life self?
- Are there aspects of your higher self that explain feelings or represent changes you have tried to make in this life? Dyeing your hair blonde when you have always been a brunette, using a straightener on naturally curly hair, excessive tanning, wearing high heels for the sake of being taller, dressing in a non-contemporary style, dressing in a style of a different culture, or wearing gender neutral or opposite-gender clothing. While it is not about doing something once or twice, if it is a regular occurrence, these are all examples of behaviors people feel consistently compelled to do to make themselves appear how they are outside of this lifetime. Without realizing why, many people for at least part of their life here will try to emulate some version of their higher self, or even their last-life self, if they have a strong subconscious connection to that aspect of themselves.
- Record direct questions asked and answers received during this meditation.

INTERCONNECTED
Coralee

In the meditation where I was meeting with my higher self, I was shown connections between Kabbalah, weight loss, house remodeling, writing, and poker. Through the meditation, I learned that all these diverse elements of my life had both spiritual and material associations, and that their lessons overlapped. Even the fact that I had been sensing that my kitchen needed to have Celtic designs stenciled in it, as part of the remodeling we were doing, was part of this energy inter-connectedness. Many of the meditations have helped with both short-term and long-term insights like this.

HEALING HEART

The Healing Heart activity meditation is an opportunity for resolution and personal growth.

Materials Needed: one of the four Healing Hearts worksheets (from the online printables; samples shown on page 145); or use a blank paper, journal page, or canvas, and your choice of pens, pencils, colored pencils, markers, pastels, and/or paints.

Choose your writing or drawing medium by how much time you have or how elaborate you want to make your project. For a fully creative work, do an initial sketch during the meditation and later transfer it to illustration board or canvas for a final piece.

For this meditation, it is helpful to play background music that is inspirational or uplifting. Once your ambience is set, reflect on your paper and begin by tracing around the heart on the worksheet. If you are starting with a blank page, draw a large heart. Outside the heart, write or draw symbols of up to five things you want to detach from at this time. Once finished, inside the heart write words or draw symbols for the attributes you want to draw within or attract to yourself.

The Meditation:

When you are satisfied with your sketch, let yourself drift into meditative state. The setting will present itself, but if it is hard to focus, going through the door in your hallway and out to your personal space works well. You will find individual objects that represent each element from your drawing that you desire to attract. Visualize holding the objects in your hands, one at a time, then dissipating the object into a ball of energy. Draw this energy into yourself and absorb the light into your heart. To rid yourself of those aspects that you denoted outside of the heart on your sketch, reverse the process. Extract the light from your heart and hold it in your hands until it materializes into an object symbolizing each of those unwanted characteristics. Bury these removed objects in the ground there and leave them behind. Think of your intentions of closure and resolution as you do so. Then, as you return home, reflect upon the new energy and aspects you have drawn into yourself. Allow yourself to recognize the change within yourself and the feelings associated with this new transfer of positive energy. Feel these new ideas growing from within. Finally, relax and smile, knowing that you have initiated an optimistic change for yourself and your path.

Upon finishing your meditation, as an additional symbolic gesture, shade over the words for aspects you left behind, leaving the new ones inside the heart brighter and bolder. Add designs or doodles inside the heart to express fulfillment and joy. Display your heart somewhere it reminds you frequently of your experience or keep it in your journal for reflection at another time.

For Your Journal

Add a quick sketch in your journal of your finished healing heart.

- Write a little about the meditation setting.
- What are the words (symbols) you put outside the heart?
- In the meditation, what objects represented those things you extracted and left behind?
- What feelings did you experience with the removal of these objects?
- What are the words (symbols) you put inside the heart?
- What objects appeared as representations of those things?
- Were there certain colors important to the process of exchanging the energies?
- Are there personal symbolic or literal meanings for you behind the objects?
- How did you feel at the end of your journey?

Consider following up in a week or two after your meditation to journal about changes or occasions arise that validate your energy exchange.

Healing Hearts worksheet samples

A Note about Spirit Guides

For anyone studying spiritual awareness, inevitably the topic of *spirit guides* surfaces. While people in general have a long-established familiarity with angels, often having been exposed to stories, religious beliefs, and depictions in artwork, it is much rarer to be raised with an understanding of our spirit guides. Briefly, spirit guides are spiritual beings who have led previous human lives. We are partnered through soul agreement as they watch over us in this life, guiding, comforting, and encouraging us.

Although we may have multiple guides that help us, the one of priority is your *highest guide* or *lifetime guide.* This guide is with you for the whole of your life. Likely, it is someone you have known in a different lifetime that you spent together or is otherwise a light being that you have profound respect for on the other side. This guide is the one and only that has access to your life plan. He or she knows specifically what intentions and purpose your soul carries. Your highest guide is able to work as a go-between for all other guides, so if you decide to explore this part of your spiritual self, plan to connect with this guide. In forming a bond, it is crucial to be able to discern him or her with clarity and assurance.

Some people have specialized spirit guides for healing, and if you learn through your highest guide that you do have a separate *healing guide*, you may wish later to build a working relationship with that being, too. It is beneficial especially for those who work in health-related fields.

Other guides come in and out of our lives for other reasons, often temporarily. They work without a need to communicate directly; we usually do not realize they are there, helping us with specific events, challenges, or concepts we are trying to grasp. You might sense there is someone new around at times of transition, growing a relationship, awaiting the birth of a child, moving to a new career, or learning a new spiritual skill. Rely on your highest guide to know if it is in your best interest to connect with the new guide, and to make the introductions if that is the case.

While it is not imperative to build a relationship or to have definitive communication with any spirit guide, it is typical for a person who is expanding their awareness to have experiences with them, anticipated or not. Guides sometimes let us know they are around by calling our name just as we are waking. Often, they try to send us signs and messages through synchronicity.

Aside from establishing communication through signs, meditation is the best way for someone to meet their spirit guide. While there are other ways to grow the bond, everyone is capable of meditating. Meeting a guide is not to be approached frivolously and timing is key. You know you are ready to take this step if you already have some awareness of your guide's presence. When they know it will benefit you to work with them, they will be persistent.

If the idea of having a spirit guide is unsettling to you, if you are afraid, or if you do not have confidence in your ultra-sensory abilities enough to meditate easily, then hold off on meeting your guides. There is no rush. They will be waiting when you are ready. Forcing a relationship with a guide that is not due to be cultivated does not work anyway. Consider using the meditation to connect with your higher self instead. For some, that is all you will ever need to do. All meditations that suggest connecting with a spirit guide are modifiable to read, "higher self."

For those who are prepared for the next step of meeting your guide, the meditation that follows is just for you.

YOUR HIGHEST GUIDE

The intention of this meditation is to introduce your highest spirit guide or *lifetime guide*. Being comfortable with meditation will greatly help the quality of your experience when you decide you are ready to meet your spirit guide. It is essential to have had successful results with *Your Personal Space* meditation (page 58) before trying this one. If, for any reason, you do not feel secure or grounded as you begin, wait until another day. It is better to be discerning than to press the matter.

Passing through the familiar first door on the right in your hallway, head out on the trail to get to the bridge. As you walk along, taking in nature with your ultra-senses, look for something you would like to give to your guide as a little gift and token of gratitude.

When you arrive at the bridge, rather than crossing it, you will find a small watercraft moored there...a rowboat, a canoe, a paddleboat, a gondola, or perhaps even a raft. Take this to float on the river, which progressively grows and widens the further you travel until it comes into a large bay. Where the river meets the bay, is a landing where you can stop.

From the landing, look for the natural rock formation tunnel that has eroded into the surrounding cliffside. Passing through this tunnel will lead you into a safe, open cove along one side of the bay and this is where you will meet your highest guide. To get there, however, you will need to leap-of-faith your way through the tunnel as the sand stops short and there is presumably deep water spanning the length of the tunnel. When you are ready, make your first leap, and as you do so, trust that a large, flat red stone will emerge to catch you as you land. Repeat this leaping process to traverse the length of the tunnel, each new stone coming up to catch you being a higher level of color—orange, yellow, green, blue, and purple. When you finally make the last jump, it will be onto the cool, beautiful, white sand beach off the cove.

Walk out a little way onto the beach to get your bearings. You can then invite your highest guide to meet you. You will initially see a very luminescent orb approaching. As it does, the features of your guide become gradually clearer until you can see their physical represent-tation. The first time you meet, it can be difficult to see your guide plainly due to the intense brightness, so if you distinguish small characteristics and little else, do not worry. They have so much energy it is a lot to attune to all at once. You will be able to spend as much time as you like here to communicate and hear messages. Any variance of perception will not influence the opportunity. Be sure to ask what name to call him by, or ask how to best connect with her in the future. Offer your guide the gift you brought along and say your goodbyes, knowing you may return to reconnect whenever you like.

Use the same rainbow-colored stones to leap back through the tunnel in reverse, taking your boat then to the bridge and your trail back to the hallway. Though you will close your door behind you as you go, know that you have made an indelible connection with your guide. It is the promise of a long and loving friendship.

The possibilities for communicating with your guide are limitless now. When you want to meet up again, you are always able to come back to the beach on the bay.

For Your Journal

- Before you arrived at the bridge in your meditation, what gift did you find to bring to your guide? What does it mean to you?
- Does the type of watercraft you find have special meaning to you? Describe the process of taking the boat to the shoreline and then leaping through the tunnel to the cove.
- Write about meeting your spirit guide. Add details about light and emotion. What are you able to perceive about the guide's appearance? Include the conversation or communication you share.
- Did you learn a name to call him or her? If you are not 100% certain about the name, you can always ask for a sign of confirmation or correction. It is a rewarding validation. If you still are not positive, trust that what you need will come when the timing is right. Until then you can always call upon your guide by whatever name you choose—they know if you are intending to address them.
- Include other information about your meditation that is pertinent for following up with in a subsequent session.

DANCING WITH REYD
Donelle

One night when I came home from Heather's Presence of Light class, I decided to do a meditation with the intention of meeting up with my guide.

I started out by going down a hallway and out my door to the right. As usual, my lion (my totem) was there waiting for me when I stepped outside. I started down my path with my lion by my side. I felt peaceful and relaxed. There was a slight breeze, it felt nice, and I was not the least bit chilly. Up ahead I saw my guide, Reyd. He smiled and held out his hands toward me. When I put my hands in his we were suddenly in San Francisco swing dancing in the street. We did not talk at all. We smiled, laughed, and danced. When I came out of the meditation, I had the song Jump, Jive an' Wail *stuck in my head. Right away I knew that I had truly experienced a past life memory. I have never been to San Francisco in this life, so how else would I know that was where I was in my meditation? Amazing.*

UNCONDITIONAL LOVE
Coralee

In general, I think I am not a person who took easily to meditating. My mind has a spinning quality that can make it hard to quiet down and calm. Most of the meditations we did throughout the workshops worked for me because it was more a

153

matter of journey and focus. Probably my most profound meditation was meeting with my spirit guide. It was very emotional, connecting to him, but also in learning about our relationship. When I asked him why he was willing to take on the task of guiding me, he said that he had been my child in a previous life and that I had died during the labor. Since I had sacrificed to give him life, he was sacrificing to help me in mine.

MEDITATION to CONNECT with YOUR HEALING GUIDE

Although this meditation appears sequentially to the meditation for meeting Your Highest Guide, it is recommended that you develop a rapport with your lifetime guide before pursuing this meditation. It will help you in being able to discern between the two guides, if you postpone this meditation until the timing calls for it.

For a small number of people, your highest guide may in fact also be your healing guide, which is something you will learn only by connecting with him or her and by growing that relationship. At a minimum, you should have done enough work with your highest guide to know if this is the case or not.

The Meditation:

Beginning in your familiar hallway, for this meditation only, go through the third door on the right. As you pass through the door, you will enter an expansive, bright white room. There is a large table in one area of the room and you will be able to sit there and talk with your highest guide (lifetime guide) once he has entered through a separate doorway into the room. Your highest guide will introduce you to your healing guide, assuming that healing is not a task delegated to your highest guide, and the three of you may discuss current issues with your physical and emotional well-being or specific questions or concerns you have. Also, do not disregard questions or healing aspects relevant to your spiritual body if you have them.

Some other possibilities for this meditation are to:

⊚ Ask how your guide can help you with healing while you sleep. Is there anything you can do to better facilitate this common healing time?

⊚ Ask about which foods you most need at this point in your life or about other dietary issues.

⊚ Ask if you are lacking specific essential vitamins? Are there dietary supplements to consider or to ask your traditional physician about?

⊚ Ask if there are physical activities that you should consider trying. Ask about the effectiveness of your current exercise program. What kinds of activities best serve your body specifically, at this point in your life?

⊚ Ask about food allergies and intolerances. Is there a way to counteract them or to recover fully?

⊚ Ask if you have any misconceptions about your health. Are you unaware of or avoiding anything?

⊚ If you have specific health concerns, ask if certain holistic treatments are a successful (or adverse) pairing with your traditional medical treatments.

*Do NOT presume to follow advice gleaned from this meditation without first discussing it with your primary care physician. *

Meditation add-on:

If you would like to do a longer healing session, on the other side of the room there is a futuristic body-scanning machine. While standing in front of it, it creates a mirror image of you. The screen image will light up segments to indicate areas of concern. Since it mirrors you, you can see where the problems are and which of those are interconnected, or which are root causes to problems and not merely the symptoms. Following the scan, there is an opportunity to discuss the scan results with your healing guide.

It is also possible, if you are open to it, that your healing guide, and perhaps other guides if needed to assist, will bring you to the healing table for an energy healing session. Your guide will let you know your options and you of course always have the choice of what you would like to participate in, or how much time you want to take for your meditation session.

For Your Journal

◎ Describe or sketch the healing room you visit.
◎ Record the names or descriptions of the guides and other light beings who are present.
◎ What questions did you ask during your session and what information or help was provided?
◎ Did ideas come up that were unexpected or new to you?
◎ If you do the healing add-on, be sure to write about your experience and if you are supposed to have a follow-up session. If so, record when you plan to do this and be sure to come back to it then, through another meditation session.
◎ If you discovered potentially helpful health information or suggestions for healing, make a separate, detailed list to take with you to your next doctor's appointment. That way you will not forget to inquire about an important matter.

THERE TO HELP
O.

My guides showed themselves to me last night. They held my hands and gave me a feeling of the emotions with which they are trying to help me. I was able to see glimpses of faces previously blurred out. I felt supported and not alone.

YOUR ANIMAL GUIDE

Just as we all have spirit guides, we also have animal guides or *totems* that are with us on our life's journey to assist us with their special wisdoms. Before you begin, invite your main animal spirit to join you on this meditative journey. Doing so enables you to see who this guide is, and then to be able to communicate and discover their special connection to you.

Using *The Hallway* as your starting point, go through the first door on the right. Continue walking this well-known path until you come to the fork. In the past, you have gone off to the left, but this time you will follow along the trail that leads to the right. As you walk, you may find that the path narrows or is overgrown with foliage, but venture onward until you reach a clearing. Especially on a first visit here, you will want to familiarize yourself with the area. Take in the sounds, sights, and smells. Is the area completely enclosed? Is there an aspect of varied terrain or even of climate? Is there a water source? When you are ready, find a comfortable place to sit down. Observe each type of animal that presents itself to you, even if they do not approach you directly.

As a side note, be open to every possible creature. Animal guides can be of any species and any size (including insects and protozoa). They may even be extinct or mythical creatures. Do not exclude anything you see. If you are unsure what kind of animal a certain one is, all you have to do is ask telepathically and use your ultra-senses to listen for the response. Be specific. For example, rather than accepting "bird," center your perception to see if you are looking at a wren, a sparrow, or a waxwing. Is that small animal a weasel, raccoon, or a civet? When interpreting the most accurate symbolism, it does make a difference.

One animal that approaches you remains with you once all the others have gone. This is your primary animal guide. In the same way as working with your spirit guides, you are free to have a telepathic conversation and ask questions of this guide, although it is a more rudimentary experience. Ask if there is a name to call her by, as you may not be at a point to recognize your totem by their energy yet. As totems, animals guide us by surrounding us with the wisdom of their strengths, natural abilities, and instincts.

An important awareness to come away from this experience with is what your animal's purpose is in guiding you. Ask questions such as, "What wisdoms are you guiding me with at this time?" When you are finished posing questions, express your gratitude to your guide and then return from your meditation by following the path from the clearing back to the hallway, letting the scene dissipate.

For Your Journal

◎ Describe your clearing, including those aspects of the terrain, climate, flora, and such, mentioned earlier.

◎ Is there a water source? If so, describe how the water appears using a few adjectives (expansive, turbulent, calm, cool, blue, dark, deep, choppy, flowing). The qualities of the water, should they change from one session to the next, provide symbolic insights to you, as water relates to our emotions.

- Could you see the sky, or did trees or a land formation obstruct it?
- Record the animals that you saw, in the order you viewed them (whether they approach you or not).
- Which animal remains with you in the end?
- Does this animal have any distinguishing marks or characteristics?
- Did you learn its name?
- What is the wisdom your totem is sharing with you?
- Were other messages shared?
- Refer to the *Quick-Check Animal Symbolism Guide* (page 270) for insights on the significance of animals you encountered during your meditation.

RAINBOW STAIRS II

Like the Rainbow Stairs I Meditation, all you will see, when you let your vision clear, is a staircase lit softly with red light. As you begin to climb the stairs, the lights will fade into the ascending colors of lights, which correspond with the chakras. Climbing will be effortless and invigorating, even if you are one who has difficulty with stairs in daily life. As you are walking up the stairs, one of the lights will reveal a wider landing leading off to the right. You can walk from the staircase landing into the adjoining room, which it leads toward, feeling safe and comfortable. Take time to survey the room and whatever you see, smell, or hear within it. As you look around, find a place to sit, unless you prefer standing still awhile. Allow the color of light on that level to surround and fill you with warmth and healing, simultaneously releasing impurities, tension, or emotions that have caused an imbalance in the corresponding chakra of your body.

When you are ready, leave this level to continue climbing the light staircase, stopping at other levels revealing a landing similar to the first. While there may be only one landing, if there are more, repeat the same energy restoring process at each, for the different chakras to absorb that color of light.

At the top of the stairwell, as the light becomes a pure white, fully surround yourself in this glorious energy.

Exit through the door you find on that level to return from your meditation, allowing the scene to fade behind you.

For Your Journal

○ Write down your healing experience, noting which landings appeared to you, the colors involved, and the healing process you went through.

○ If you feel that specific blockages or emotions were released, record your awareness or feelings on this afterward.

○ How do the release of blockages and the concurrent healing help you with certain events to come or with goals that you are trying to achieve?

LIFE, CREATIVITY, & NATURE

This meditation for growth and understanding is appropriate for either one longer sitting, or three shorter, separate sittings, exploring one pathway each visit.

Clarity of your meditative sight will reveal a path to you. When you walk along, you will come to a stop where three things block the path, stopping you from proceeding onto one of the three forked trails beyond the objects. The first item is a plant; the second, a vase; the third, an animal. Choose which direction you would like to traverse, and then go to the object in your way. Notice the details of it. As you are inspecting it, a guide will appear to you to lead you along the pathway beyond the object. Bring the object that corresponds to your chosen route along with you to the destination point. The scene and imagery you see at the end of each trail will have significant meaning. Knowledge will be imparted to you regarding life (the plant), art and creativity (the vase), and nature (the animal). Leave the object there unless guided to do otherwise.

You can return down the trail to pick up your next item and venture another trail, or come back to this place in another meditation session. If you opt to continue on, carefully observe the details. You may have a new guide to lead you on each of the different routes, or the same guide may be present for the entire course. Be open to the presence of your guide or guides when you are ready to proceed. To complete your adventure, return home along the main path.

For Your Journal

◎ Describe the setting of your meditation.

◎ Record details about the plant, the vase, and the animal. Are there any personal ties to these things of which you immediately are aware?

◎ Which path did you first take? Which guide, by name or description, accompanied you?

◎ Record the information and knowledge you acquired throughout your journey. If you opt to explore all three routes, of course include details about the entire experience.

◎ In what practical ways will you apply these ideas in coming days?

ONE SALAMANDER and a BIT of MAGIC
Heidi

I began the meditation walking along the path until I came to where it branched into three separate paths. The middle path contained a vase that appeared to me as a silver pitcher with a handle. I picked it up, and there appeared a woman in a white robe that tied at the waist. She took the pitcher from me and we walked down the path for a while. We did not talk. The landscape was dry with a slight rise on either side of the hard path. It had the feeling and colors of the southwest. Eventually, we came to the edge of a cliff. Below in the valley was a small city. The woman turned to me and poured a drop of white fluid out of the pitcher onto my head. After she did this, I found myself flying down to the city. I came to an apartment building and then to a particular window. I went through the window and inside was an older woman lying in bed. She was in the last stage of life and would soon pass away. I gave her a kiss on the cheek and suddenly found myself back on the path.

Then, I turned to my left and there in the middle of the path was a large fern in a pot. I picked the pot up and cradled it in my arms the best I could. It was quite large. A very happy little old man came to get me, and we set off down a green winding path. This path led to the ocean. We settled in on the beach and the man took out a large poster-sized piece of paper as well as paints, colored pencils and pens. We spent some time drawing and writing, and goofing around. It was very playful. I enjoyed my time with him. We then took the fern and found a spot up toward the path in a rocky but green area and we planted the fern. We packed it in with dirt, but also with beautiful blue and green sea glass that sparkled and glittered. Then, we leisurely returned to the fork in the road.

As I stood looking to my right at the final path, I felt a deepening of the moment. On the path, I saw a salamander that I walked over to and placed him on my shoulder. I was waiting for a figure to appear. After waiting a little while, I started down the path on my own. A man in a brown robe was a short distance from the start, sitting behind a tree facing down the path. He stood up as I approached and said he was waiting for me to take the initiative to find him. We quietly made our way down the path. Suddenly the path transformed, and we were standing in a vault. It felt like a combination of a bank safe and a sacred cave. It was a man-made space, but it connected to the sacred. We stood quietly and the man—who appeared as a monk—said to me that I need to be willing to seek and that I had to be willing to be *patient. The salamander on my shoulder put its head up and gently bit my ear. I was instantly again at the crossroads and the meditation was over.*

My interpretation of the first step of the meditation was that it had to do with the art of healing. I know the vase represents art and creativity. Recently, I was contemplating that my role as a nurse lives in the realm of art more than in the science of nursing. My skills lie in offering presence and other things that, outside of my clinical skills, can be hard to define, but that are deeply meaningful to me and to the people for whom I care.

In the second step of the meditation, I reviewed the importance of play, lightheartedness, relaxation, and connection, as well as a little magic symbolized by the sparkly sea glass that I used in planting the fern.

After the meditation, I looked up the symbolic meaning of the salamander. This is not an animal I think of often. The first interpretation that I found stated that it was a symbol of intuition. The feeling that I had from the third step, with the salamander and the monk, was the need for me to work, with intention and patience, on things like this meditation that get me in touch with my intuitive self.

RE-CREATING YOUR SPACE

At the apex of a small hill is a tiny building, perhaps a small house, cottage, cabin, or yurt. This is where you will find yourself as your vision becomes sharp and clear.

Briefly, think of a concern or blockage you are facing. You have heard the phrase "putting up walls," with regard to psychologically protecting oneself from others trying to get to know them. The building you see is quite similar in a symbolic way, as it represents blocks and comfort levels fabricated around yourself. This becomes a barrier to your emotions, your creativity, and your spirituality. It hinders your connection with your higher self and spirit guides. Whatever it is that you feel closed off to right now, you will be able to open yourself to again here in this place.

As you approach, look to find your hidden key. When you retrieve it, go, and unlock the door. What do you feel and see as you enter the space? What you will do next is a symbol of your own choosing in the interest of opening, brightening, cleaning, and thoroughly transforming this space into a wondrous and magical place. It is not necessary to dissolve the walls representing barriers, because we all deserve to feel secure. Rather, find a healthy balance by altering what appears to be sealed or rigid, to be passable or inviting for energy to flow freely in and out of this space. Open the windows and let the sun inside. Find paints or supplies to refurbish or clean. Use the items from the storage area to redecorate. Whatever it is that you would like to do, re-create the building. Make it a better, more complete expression of yourself. Consider incorporating components of all your senses.

When you are finished, leave your space open and unlocked. Take the key with you. Anytime you feel you need to return to this space, you are free to do so. Additionally, should you ever begin to wonder about blockages recurring in life, quickly visualize your key as a reminder of your new, magical, and open space.

Returning here is possible whenever you want to revisit the meditation. It is always available to you to modify and update further. You can use it as a getaway for a peaceful meditation setting, especially when you want to reflect on openness, your connection to the world, or self-awareness.

For Your Journal

- What is your blockage or concern?
- What did the building look like when you first saw it?
- Where did you find your hidden key? Is there any significance in this that you are aware?
- What did you do to re-create your space?
- What was most difficult and/or most simple about the experience?
- How did you feel upon concluding the meditation?

LYRICAL MEDITATION

Sometimes we do not really have a question in mind, but we simply want or need a message, regardless of whether struggling with a challenge or perfectly content in the moment. This music-based activity meditation is perfect for gathering what it is we most need to hear.

Materials to prepare for the Lyrical Meditation are paper, pen/pencil, and a set of song lyric quotations. For your personal use and convenience, there is a free Song Lyric Cut-Outs printable available to you online (see *Meditation Materials & Resources*, page 257).

If you opt to make your own set of song lyric quotes instead, use your private music collection or an online source to gather a set of quotations. A Web search for "famous lyrics quotes" produces good resources. You will need at least ten quotations from songs, written on small pieces of paper or printed and then cut apart. The more lyrics the better however, as it will give you a more random pool to choose from when you do your meditation. Any lyrics can work, but those especially insightful, are ones that deal with common life themes or those that hold some sort of universal wisdom. Essentially, you are looking for lyrics to provide a broad range of possible messages. You could include lyrics like, "*No, they can't take that away from me,*" from Billie Holiday, "*You know I love you, I'll always be true,*" from The Beatles, or the Stephen Foster verse, "*Beautiful dreamer, wake unto me. Starlight and dewdrops are waiting for thee.*"

Once you have the lyrics written on paper, fold them in half or quarters. Mix them up on a table top or in a bowl, then select one, two, or three of the lyrics at random, keeping them in the order that you draw them. After you have chosen the ones you are going to use, you can look at them. It is a good idea to record the verses into your journal before you begin the meditation, or if you do not want to re-use the chosen lyrics, tape them directly into your journal instead.

The Meditation:

Deliberate on each line so you will remember the lyrics in the order that you selected them, without having to break your concentration to look back at the papers. When you have them all in mind, shift your perspective to a relaxed state of darkness and calm. Your breathing regulates to a peaceful, even rate.

Imagine a wonderful outdoor amphitheater open entirely for you. Perhaps it will turn out to be somewhere you have attended a concert or play in the past, but it could also be a completely unfamiliar location. It may even turn out to be a place you dream of traveling to someday. Because there are abundant possibilities, try to let the setting unfold for you rather than pre-determining it.

In this setting, find a place you want to sit or stand to focus on your first line of music. You have complete access to the seating area, the stage, or backstage, so wander wherever you like. Within the meditation, you can sing the verse, hum it, say it, or simply hold the words in your thoughts. You do not physically have to sing it for this meditation to work. Though, if you are so compelled, sing out strong. Listen for the messages that come back to you in reply. Watch to see if other activities take place in front of you. Discern ultra-sensory changes and accept emotional meanings that come up.

If you selected a second or third song lyric at the start, you have the option to move to a different spot in the amphitheater for each one, or to stay put as you ponder them. While you are there, take special note of little extras that intrigue you. These features often hold symbolic significance or are a sign in some way. Examples include a playbill on a seat, a set design, a theater prop or musical instrument left standing out, the color of the curtains, or a candy wrapper blowing past. The most unusual details may bring you great insights. Even if you do not understand it immediately, it does not mean that it will not tie into a moment in your life that occurs weeks later.

When you are finished with the selected lyrics and you have received your messages, make your way to the amphitheater exit. Everything will fade and your consciousness will shift back to home as you pass through the venue gates.

For Your Journal

◎ List the song quotations you selected in order, with space between them for meditation details and corresponding messages. Upon first reading them, did you have immediate claircognizant insights about any of the phrases?

◎ Write about the beginning of your meditation, the amphitheater, and the atmosphere.

- Describe the process of focusing on the lyrics, including detail, like where you chose to sit or stand, and what you experienced in those moments.
- Record direct messages you received about the lyrics.
- What, if any, extra aspects did you notice and what do you feel are the meanings, messages, or significance behind them? Make note of the point during the meditation you saw these additional elements as well, as the timing may correlate directly to the lyrics engaging you at that instant.
- Do you see how the lyrics you selected connect to a certain situation in your life? Do they hold individual meanings? What personal events have transpired the need for this guidance?

For a Group Meditation:

If you are doing this meditation as a group activity, you will need at least six lyrics per person participating. Use the online printable, but feel free to add to the selection of lyrics by making your own Song Lyric Cut-Outs. Again, select lyrics across all genres of music, because even if it is a piece you are not familiar with, or if it does not play to your taste, that does not mean it will not bring an evocative message or synchronicity for someone else in the group.

Another idea to further engage the group is to ask each person in advance to prepare and bring along six song lyric quotations. Ask for lyrics that have been personally meaningful to them at some point in life. Be sure they understand that individual lines are needed, not song lyrics in their entirety. They should know that in choosing which lyrics to contribute, they are looking for a message that holds meaning; were it found inside a fortune cookie, it would satisfy in a direct or symbolic way. (There is not a lot of takeaway with *"tweedle lee dee dee dee, tweedle lee dee dee"*).

When everyone gathers for the meditation session, provide matching papers to record the lyrics. Use the fill-in printable, if you would like (see page 266). The name of the artist or band should be included on each for the benefit of the person who selects the paper. Whether they are familiar with the tune or not, they can look it up later, if interested.

Add the contributed lyrics to the pool or use them solely. While the participants may not end up selecting any lyrics of their own, sharing the meaningful lyrics is a little gift in connecting with each other. It may also bring about some wonderful discussion following your meditations, when everyone is able to share their meditation experiences, but also be able to speak as to why they contributed a certain quotation.

VIEWING ROOM

Think of something you want to understand or change about yourself or your life, or as an alternative, think of a decision you face. Write about this at the top of your journaling page, and then proceed with your routine and meditative relaxation. Doing so will give confirmation and clarity to your intention.

On this meditation journey, you find yourself in a room filled with many, many labeled cubbies holding various containers. Find the cubby that is right for you now, the one drawing you in, or standing out in a certain way. Among other possibilities, the label, design, or color may influence your choice. Take the container out of the cubby and bring it with you to the adjacent area, where the viewing rooms are located.

Choose a vacant room to use. Inside the container you are holding is a recording to watch. This recording will reveal to you the roots of what it is you would like to change, or the underlying matters of the decision. You may see critical events from your life that have led up to this point, or even elements of a past life, so do not be startled by what you learn here as you are screening your recording. Take an observational, objective viewpoint, in the interest of absorbing the most detail possible. Be assured that a more complete view of the topic is going to provide you with helpful understanding and knowledge that will enable you to move forward more smoothly.

After the initial phase of the viewing, you will be shown ideas of how to change or release this issue. It is probable that one or more of your spirit guides will be present to help you in this process. Realize that gaining precise solutions is unlikely, because outside tampering with our free will is forbidden. Instead, the viewing process clarifies information. It reveals the array of choices, especially for ideas previously unconsidered. The process also brings to light the understanding of what is in our best interest. Receiving guidance enough to enable decision-making is possible. Do not forget to communicate and ask questions of your guides while in meditation, especially if you need further clarification.

When you are done with your viewing session, return the recording back to its container and leave it on the returns shelf. Come back here through meditation whenever you want to view another insightful film. Until then, take a seat and allow everything to fade into darkness, becoming again conscious of your breathing.

For Your Journal

○ What life aspect, change, or decision was the intention for your meditation?
○ How did the cubby and viewing rooms appear? Was the setting contemporary, futuristic, or long-ago?
○ Tell about the cubbies and the recording. Onto what format of media is this life record stored? Is this format obsolete, modern, or futuristic? (Perhaps there is a sign or message for you in this detail alone.)
○ Describe your experience in the media viewing room.
○ Did a specific guide assist you?

◎ How are you instructed to resolve or alter the situation? Is there action to be taken? Make special note of the information you receive for future reference.

A PRODUCTIVE PERSPECTIVE
Heather

My intention for my first viewing room meditation was to try to learn about my challenging relationship with money. What I saw on film were problems that began in another life, being a wealthy person of great entitlement who never had to think about money, followed by a second lifetime where I lived a very impoverished existence. I was then shown how all this was compounded in my early years of this life, essentially being raised to be afraid of money, never being shown how to understand or manage it. My parents outright avoided discussing or teaching us kids about money, saving, spending, or any topic related whatsoever.

My spirit guide showed me that I am able to alter my perspective by seeing money coming into my life as something beautiful. In this part of the meditation, I saw a dollar bill as it folded into a lovely origami bird, which then morphed and blossomed into a deep red rose. It is clear that changing my perspective will help me greatly to see money and finances not as something to fear or worry over, but to see it with the same reverence and gratitude I hold for nature and the outdoors.

I can't say that making the change is easy or absolute, but I have received validation and positive outcomes from the universe in responsive ways each time I avoid falling back into the same old perspective. Over a longer period of time it could prove very productive and stabilizing for my life.

TAROT MEDITATION

To do this insight meditation, you will need a standard, well-illustrated tarot deck. If you do not have one available, most oracle decks with detailed art will work in the same way.

First, sort through your deck and select out your favorite card or the one you find most appealing in the moment and set it aside. Next, shuffle your deck. Asking your spirit guide or higher self to help, listen for the first number that pops into your head when you ask, "Which number card do I need?" With the deck face down, count from the top card downward until you get to the number you heard, and take out that card. Set your deck aside and hold on to the two cards you have chosen.

The first card (your favorite) is the scene for your meditation. As you go into your meditative state, you will see yourself "walking into" the card, which becomes the setting for your meditation.

The second card is a snapshot. It is about your life in this moment in time. If it has positive overtones to you, it depicts what you need in the moment. It can be about what you are coming into, or what you are drawing into your life. If the card has negative overtones to you, it indicates what is important to overcome or rid yourself of on this occasion.

Once you go into the meditation, you will find guidance in this unique setting. You can explore, but do not forget to concentrate on the task, focusing on the imagery and ideas of the second card. Allow insights to surface, which will aid your present circumstances. Are there obvious or hidden messages in the correlation between the setting and your second card? What should you be aware of in overcoming an obstacle or drawing aspects to you? When you have received your messages, thank those who helped guide you, then, step back out of your card setting.

For Your Journal

◎ What card did you choose as your favorite and why?

◎ Which number did you hear (or see, or feel) to draw for your second?

◎ In your meditation, how did the first card come to life for you as the meditation setting?

◎ Which card was the second that you drew from the deck? What were your initial impressions? Were there any positive or negative overtones?

◎ What guidance did you receive regarding the card you drew?

SERENDIPITY
Marie D.

Beautiful children dancing on the card drew me into the image. The assignment was to pick my favorite card to represent my "scene" when in fact I drew one that directly mirrored my life. Three beautiful children, dancing and holding hands, represented who I am now. Love, family, tin-foiled hearts hang-

ing above, all symbolically reflecting my life here and now. Immediately when I realized this, it opened my eyes, for this painted my "favorite" place being the reality of what I currently experience. Tears filling my eyes blurred the image together, as tingles of energy raced through my body.

A time of uncertainty and longing immerses me. There is certain emptiness, a realization that is misunderstood, filling me with stress and fear. This beautiful moment now brought my perfect life to clarity. A card...any scene that I could pick... attracted me to the one that parallels my life in many dimensions. I close my eyes and I am still here in this small messy living room, sounds of children, exhaustion and happiness cascading through me. The childlike passion of the image, the innocence, the nature and roses symbolizing Divine worth dive deep down to touch the soul. The delicate lace in the background brings me back before this life. All of which is encompassed by a heart of love and the gentle breeze of life tickling the senses.

The three children are *a younger version of my sisters and me. The three children* are *my three children. The three children* are *the past, present, and future dancing together in time. In all three cases, the eldest girl draws me in, connects to me. That girl is me, my past, my daughter. Our souls dance as the same, caring for each other and echoing innocent joys. Five years old, my daughter said to me this week, "We are secret soul sisters, Mom." I now see it serendipitously in this scene; it is a connection I have always longed to unearth. This is not only the six-of-hearts card that I drew; this is a scene of my life.*

As the next card enters my vision, I cannot breathe, my heart catches in my chest. A cold shiver runs down my arms as I hold the Temperance card in my hand. As though picked from the stars, the Universe fits it perfectly into what I need, what I seek, what I cannot grasp mentally. Reality dances in and out of my illusions. I second-guess what I am, how I am connected, and what my calling is. My eyes draw into the pouring water as it cascades into my being. I still cannot comprehend entirely, how this card symbolizes what I need...what I am coming into. Images of time, wisdom, peace, solitude, connection encircle my spirit. Heaven intertwines with earth as the tree of life draws me in. Alone the tree calls to me to understand, to find peace. I seek to go deeper into the understanding I have covered with these shallow distractions. I need to listen and to open myself to all that there is. To trust.

THE SHOPPE

Taken back in time, this meditation is a visit to a quaint old shop. The store may present itself in a few ways, as an alchemist's, a trading post, or even an antique shop. However the setting appears to you personally, it will be a safe, comfortable, and magical place whenever you use this meditation.

Upon arriving, feel free to explore outside the building. While you are looking around, spot the bag of coins left there for you to use. Once you have this, you will be able to venture inside.

Although there are lots of interesting and perhaps obscure objects to be found, look for the ornate glass case, which displays a selection of unique and extraordinary items. The shopkeeper will help you with any enticing objects you wish to inspect more closely. Additionally, take the opportunity to ask questions either of the shopkeeper, of your spirit guides, or of your higher self, as to what each piece is for, and about its potential to help you.

Choose which items you would like to purchase and bring them back with you. If you have coins left over, you can put the bag back in its little hiding place where you found it, or hold on to it to use on your next journey to the old shoppe.

For Your Journal

- Describe the shop.
- Is the place at all familiar to you? What makes it resonate with your spirit?
- Where did you discover your bag of coins? Is there anything symbolic for you about that?
- What items could you choose from in the case?
- What did you opt to purchase on this visit?
- What purpose does your selected item hold?
- Is there an item you left in the case despite a fascination with it? (Keep this in mind for meditating another time, as it may be something you need in the future).

SCALE MEDITATION

The scene for this meditation centers on an oversized, classic-style weighing scale. Whether it is a modern setting, or in the Renaissance, how the environment appears to you personally is as it should be.

One side of the scale holds several rocks. These rocks represent burden. If you look closer, you will see inscribed words representative of responsibilities, challenges you face, and burden you carry. The other side of the scale has much more varied natural objects on it, other than rocks. This side of the scale includes and symbolizes positive, constructive, intellectual, and spiritual aspects in your life.

Choose how to balance your scale.

Both sides to the scale are necessary as part of the human experience. If the scale appears to be reasonably balanced from the start, you may inspect it to see if the representations on each side equate the balance you would like to maintain.

Although it is up to the individual, a modification to the weights is recommended when there is a grave imbalance between the two sides. There are three ways to achieve equilibrium. First, discarding something you want to be finished with or to disconnect from is an option. Second, adding newfound elements or objects to one side or the other adjusts the scale. Search around the scene you are in to find these items to use. Third, removing a piece from one side of the scale and transforming it into something that fits in the opposite side is the last option. This could easily be a rock taken from the burden side, which is transformed and moved to the positive side when you take an optimistic, new perspective on it. Or, an object on the positive side representing what you have been resistant to changing, which now needs to be addressed or overcome. This you opt to move to the *burden* side. It is all entirely up to you. Your guides or higher self will be able to help you determine the changes in your best interest to create a better balance for yourself, so remember to ask questions if you are not certain how to level your scale.

As a last note, do not assume that those rocks on the burden side are "bad." They are simply illustrative of what you are working on, and of what comes with human challenge and experience. Arriving on the scene to find the burden side of the scale flat on the ground may be a tiny sign for the person trying to be superhuman. Leveling your scale is about gaining awareness of how many facets to life are cycling all at once. It is a way to realize what works best for you, what can change, and sometimes, of what you might be able to let go. Whether you finish with the scale leveled evenly or not, you still will come away knowing more about your work-in-progress self.

Once balanced to your liking, the scale and scene will fade from view, allowing you to return home.

For Your Journal

- Write about or diagram your scale and the scene you are in for your meditation. Include the inscriptions you read on either side of the scale.
- Explain the process you go through to balance the scale.

◎ If guides give you input on how to create balance, make some notes about their advice.

◎ Are there symbolic meanings behind the objects on the side opposite the rocks?

◎ Did aspects found on either side of the scale surprise you?

◎ Did you add one or more completely new pieces to the scale? If so, what were they and what did they represent?

◎ Was there anything you completely removed from the scale to leave behind?

◎ How do you feel upon coming out of the meditation, whether physically, spiritually, or emotionally?

◎ When you finish, how do you leave the scale? Was anything unresolved that you want to go back to address at another time?

Further journaling:

With the topic of this meditation being about balance, spend awhile contemplating that aspect of your life. Think of a time in your past when you felt that everything was harmonious. What were the elements that contributed to that? How did aspects of family, friends, health, work/ career/school, home/living situation, intellectual growth, hobbies/free time, spirituality, or finances come together? Do you remember what, if anything, felt like it was missing back then? How does all that compare to now? Are you challenged intellectually? Do you find ways to express your creativity? Are you following passions? Is there a pastime you have sacrificed for the sake of responsibilities that used to bring you more balance and happiness? How do you share of yourself and connect to others? In what ways do you acknowledge all that you are grateful for today?

Our lives are a progression, so you should not look back in such a way as to re-create the past or dwell on specifics, but rather seek out ideal situations in your present, relevant to your needs, that help you feel fulfilled. What is *your* next adventure?

WALK in SOMEONE ELSE'S SHOES

The chance encounters, the cherished friendships, the loves, the family bonds...every connection, every moment shared with another, gives us a chance to fulfill a soul agreement with another person. So how do we satisfy those agreements when there is an obstacle? How do we best honor these connections if we cannot find common ground or harmony with the other person? Meditating on the questions we have and trying to see the other person's perspective can be helpful in many instances. Through better understanding them, we can often better know what we ourselves should realize, what to act on, or how to find peace.

All you need for this meditation is to know which person you want to reflect on to learn more about your connection and to appreciate your roles and differences. If you have specific questions weighing on you, it would be a good idea to write those down in your journal before you start. Doing this sets the intention that the questions be answered in some way during your session. Note that you may not receive direct, verbatim instruction, as we generally need to live through the circumstances and use our free will to proceed. Attaining information, signs, or details to help guide you will be adequate in moving ahead.

The Meditation:

Hold your chosen person in mind as you begin your meditation, thinking, "Help me to know you and further understand our relationship." As your clarity in meditative state transpires, you will find a pair of this person's shoes on the floor in front of you.

Slip your feet into the shoes. In the way that meditation exclusively allows, they will magically fit you despite the person's actual shoe size or stature. Next? Walk. Saunter through the surroundings, scenarios, or events presented to you. Do not try to create or force a scene. Take your time and be nothing but observant. Absorb everything you can to the end that it will enable you to fully understand this person and thereby to recognize the truths of your relationship.

When you are ready to be done, respectfully remove the shoes and place them in front of you, with toes pointed toward you, so as a person standing face-to-face with you would be able to slip them back on again. You are unlikely to see the person, but in thought be sure to send your thanks and gratitude to them before you open your eyes.

For Your Journal

- Whose shoes did you chose to walk in?
- Is there a reason, event, or situation that necessitated you to try this meditation? If so, write it down so when you look back on your notes sometime in the future you will remember the impetus.
- Describe the shoes you found waiting for you. Though it is possible they resemble the person's actual shoes, a variant may bring more insights if you do some further research on the symbolism.
- Detail the experience you have while wearing the shoes.

◎ What are your thoughts on the information disclosed to you? How are you able to use this to strengthen your connection or fulfill a part of your soul agreement?

◎ Do you feel there is a gesture to make or piece to say following your meditation that will nurture your relationship?

◎ If you needed resolution, is there additional work you could do to help yourself in healing or in getting the closure you need?

◎ Consider returning to your notes in a few days to add updates or other revelations.

THE CLOCK TOWER

This meditation is an opportunity to explore *human* perceptions of time, and to understand how time plays a role in our life. For this meditation, it is set in contrast to the spiritual idea of time and the concept that on the *Other Side* there is no such thing as time, as we observe and measure it here. For simplicity sake, we are taking a "here vs. there" point of view.

However, if you must, it is an opportunity to delve into all those quantum physics questions stored up, regarding the theory that altogether time does not exist. Do not feel obligated to dive off that board too soon though, because it is an infinite sea of mind-boggling ideas and unending questions out there in the deep.

Entering into meditation, look around the area to find the clock tower. Like no ordinary structure, this clock tower has two divisions or sides to it. You will approach the "human" or "time" side, which appears to be more solid and dense. Initially, this part of the clock tower may be all that is visible. Enter through the doorway and take the stairs effortlessly to the top. From the top level, you will be able to move between the experience of time on both the "human side" and the "spiritual side."

The "spiritual side" of the clock tower is a more ethereal location, vibrating at a higher frequency and less dense level. You should be able to easily pass between the two sides as needed to explore and experience perceptions and gain insights to questions that you have.

Begin your session with the question, "What should I know about time and how I spend it in this lifetime?" Continue by asking questions you are most interested in covering. Though it is best to navigate the meditation in your own way, one approach is to ask the same questions from each side of the clock tower. Write at least two starter questions in your journal as a basis for the meditation.

Sample questions include:

- What do I forget to incorporate into each day?
- Is it important to make time for _____?
- Would it be in my best interest to _____ (meditate, be outside, connect with family, work, exercise, travel, etc.) more often?
- Would time spent on _____ help me?
- How can I make the most of _____ (a period of time—the next month, this fall, my school year)?
- How can I make more time for _____?
- How would I view _____ differently from a solely spiritual perspective?

Spend as much time as you need to address your questions or to explore the two sides of the clock tower while you acquire information. To return, venture back down the staircase and as you exit the doorway, allow the clock tower and setting to fade away.

For Your Journal

- ◎ Before you begin your meditation, record all the questions you initially intend to ask, leaving space to write the answers.
- ◎ Describe your clock tower and a bit about how it looks, feels, and smells, to detail your experience.
- ◎ What were your impressions between the human versus the spiritual sides of the clock? What differences did you feel emotionally or physically between the contrasting sides? Did one side feel more calming, hopeful, peaceful, or positive?
- ◎ Regarding the decided questions you started with, did you find commonalities between the guidance you received on either side of the clock tower?
- ◎ Remember to record all the answers to your questions and follow up in a few days with discoveries or responses to changes you notice in your life with regard to time.

Further journaling:

Spend a few moments thinking about the role time has played for you thus far in life. Choose from the following sets of prompts for more introspection and journaling to better comprehend time and its influence on you personally.

In what ways have you struggled with time or resisted it? Do you feel different about time now than you did as a teen; how so? How might a change in perspective about time be helpful or hopeful to you?

Do you remember a situation where time has been beneficial, funny, or a blessing? What is the most recent moment of Divine timing you have experienced?

Do you feel time is a hindrance? Are you a person who is generally early, on time, or late for everything? Does that work in your favor? How has this affected you or others? Is there anything you desire to change about this?

🐾 Helping Loved Ones

Some days, after being drained by demanding jobs, schedules, and responsibilities, we barely have enough left to offer anyone else beyond a compliment. Compassionately, we should deduce that all other people face the same challenges, even if they emerge in different ways. Everyone is going through something. That is what we signed up for coming into a human lifetime. It is not about going it all alone though; as humans we genuinely are in this together. Supporting another, helping a loved one, it is all one aspect of the cycle of giving and receiving we spiritually endeavor to master. If we are open, observant, and impartial to support one another, in ways that we are capable, the human experience is improved for everyone.

Assume everyone, yes, *everyone*, is doing the best that he, or she, can at any given moment. (It is not by your standard, which is between you and your higher power, just as it is between them and theirs.) We need help. (This is not to say that we should not try, or conversely, be too proud to accept aid). Others need help. (This is not to say they always make it easy to do so). Strife necessitates thoughtfulness. Problems are not unraveled by swiftly stepping in with unsolicited advice or money loans. Trying to solve a loved one's troubles for him, just because the answer seems easy or obvious, is even worse.

Being interconnected, however, how do we best honor each other's individual life paths, including the challenges they are bound to face? In many ways, it simply comes down to being present. Consider this: easy, obvious solutions are only recognizable to a person who has already lived through equivalent circumstances in this lifetime or another. That person has already had a chance to figure it out. The one who is struggling is now trying to do the same. This is why it is important for us to recognize and set aside judgment. Becoming aware of someone else's challenge brings an opportunity to do one of two things: pass judgment that it is simple to overcome and try to fix it for them, or offer to be a resource and work together with the struggling person to bring about a solution.

Several years ago at a workshop, while the students were doing an exercise, I was going around the room to help anyone that was stuck or needed extra input. As part of the activity, one student had posed a personal question regarding her young adult son and his love relationship. She had desperately been trying to help him. As mothers will relate, it is dreadful when our progeny suffers. She felt she had to intervene. She wanted to fix it for him. Those feelings though were where she was stuck on the workshop exercise. She had not done it incorrectly; she was only clouded by emotion and preconception that held her back from clearly seeing the answer she had assembled. The answer was simply that she take a step back. It was not her problem. If she plainly offered him compassion and understanding, if she told him that she had faith in him, and if she let him know that she was unconditionally available as a resource, that would be enough. It was undoubtedly difficult, but she did just that. She let him know she was *present*. About a week later, he had not only made some very mature decisions, but also changes that bettered the situation and proved to be a foundation for him and his future.

It can be heartbreaking watching someone struggle. Our first thought is reactionary, jump in and save them. Of course, it is decent and moral to offer objective advice when invited, to give a financial gift, or to support and guide someone navigating an obstacle. Yet, there are times we want to do right by others when we do not have the opportunity or the means to help in these ways. As that mother did, sometimes we should just be present and wait it out. In some cases, our hurt feelings get the best of us, so we withdraw our presence, and we wait too long. Nevertheless, we should not forget there are always things we can do. We can offer other simple, yet tremendously significant gifts freely. Five of these are the focus of the meditation that follows, *What Others Need*. It is an opportunity to deepen relationships and understanding, as you explore ways to help your loved ones.

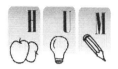

WHAT OTHERS NEED

To prepare for this meditation, you will need five small matching scraps of paper. Write one phrase per paper as follows:

> *Unconditional love*
> *Kindness*
> *Healing/Prayers*
> *Time*
> *Forgiveness or Compassion*

Fold the papers and put them aside in a little pile to draw from during the second step of the meditation.

The Meditation:

Hold onto a pen and have an open page in your journal ready. Go into a calm, lightly meditative state of mind. Ask which five people in your life (present, absent, or passed) you need to include in this meditation. As you hear their names or see impressions of them, write down their names as a list.

Once you have your list, think of the first name while selecting one of the five phrase papers you have folded up. Write the corresponding gift you can offer this person next to their name. Refold the paper and put it back in the pile. Mix them up, and thinking of the second name, select another paper. Record the second gift. Repeat this step until you have a gift next to each name you wrote down. As to be expected, some of the gifts may appear more than once.

In your meditation, you will have one or more guides to discuss with and to help you determine how you can best offer these gifts to the people you named. The scene for the meditation is not critical, so you can go to *Your Personal Space* (page 58), or instead, use this as a clairaudience-only exercise from the usual opening state of peaceful darkness. Conclude the meditation by setting intention to offer your gifts to these people. Making individual statements such as, "Margot, I offer you my gift of kindness," render it more purposeful for the days that follow.

For Your Journal

◎ If you used separate paper, transfer all the names and gifts to your journal. What are your initial thoughts and feelings about the pairings of names and gifts? Do you have reservations about any of the names or gifts on the list?

◎ Why do you believe these five people were selected as the focus of your meditation? Write about where each relationship stands, and note immediate situations or vital background story.

◎ What advice and input did you receive throughout the meditation?

◎ Are there specific, suggested ways to offer your gifts to these people?

◎ What actions are required on your part? How do you intend to fulfill your gift giving?

◎ Follow-up with adding in details should they arise over the next few weeks.

◎ For a future session, you might consider adding to the pool of choices other ways, within your power, that you are able to help others. Examples might include: offer a financial gift, accompany this person to _____, teach this person how to _____, share _____ with this person, intervene, protect or speak up for this person, and so on.

For a Group Meditation:

With a small group, make sure that the full set of five papers to select from is available to each person. They could make their own set from scrap paper provided. Otherwise, sharing one set in a little bowl that the group passes around works, too. Wait until everyone has had a turn to write the phrases down before continuing.

If there are a large number of participants, it is easiest to provide individual sets of phrase papers to speed up the process. A printable is available for convenience (see *Meditation Materials & Resources*, page 257).

The GIFT of TIME
Julia

The five people identified for my meditation were my husband, mother, father, sister, and mother-in-law. I drew out the following phrases for each one—Husband, kindness; Mother, healing/ prayers; Father, kindness; Sister, healing/prayers; and Mother-in-law, time.

When I did the meditation, I asked my guides how I could best offer the gifts to each of these people. I kept getting the same message coming back to spend more time with them. For my husband, I received the message to offer kindness by spending more time talking to him. We are both busy and work different schedules, so it is difficult to make time to sit and talk. For my mother, I got the message to offer her reassurance. She is the worrier of the family and is often concerned about others. For my father, the message was to spend more time with him. When I visit my parents, I spend the majority of the time talking with my mother, so that message made sense as well. For my sister, I knew beforehand that I would draw the healing/prayers paper, which is exactly how it happened. She has a debilitating disease and is in the middle of healing from a flare up. I was told to spend more time praying for her, as well as to spend time with her. Lastly, I drew time for my mother-in-law. She lost her husband of over 40 years last year. She is having a difficult time being alone. My message was to spend more time with her also. The messages that I received were all clear that I need to slow down in my life and spend time with those who I love.

THE CAVERN

The following meditation is ideal for seeking resolution and understanding with another person. This person has been a part of your life, either present or past, but in either instance, it is someone you do not have the option to resolve issues with face-to-face. As you settle into your meditation, send thoughts to invite this person's higher self to connect with you through this experience.

At the edge of a forest, where the tree line meets an open field of long grasses and wildflowers, there is an inconspicuous knoll. A spirit guide should lead your way. Once you discover where it is situated and you approach it, your guide will show you an entryway leading to an underground cavern. The guide will wait for you here until you return.

Descend the earthen stairway into the vast darkness. Based on a present fear, a certain challenge to undertake presents itself. Surpass and overcome your fear, in whatever way it manifests, as you move through the first chamber at the bottom of the stairs. Doing so allows you to enter the passageway to the wondrous second chamber. It is a beautiful, sacred place. Most that come here are welcomed through a certain measure of ritual and formality. Let the others present in this chamber guide you through the ceremony, which involves candle lighting, blessings, or other observances. Be open and peaceful as you participate.

Following your initial ceremony, and once seated, a "Council of Elders" will enter through another passageway. Next, brought into the chamber is the person with whom you are seeking resolution or understanding. The council speaks to you and the other person, so listen intently. Questions may be asked of you. Guidance and instruction are given. Take part in the formalities and be open to hearing honest input about your life.

When the ceremony concludes, you will be able to return by going back the same way you came in, though that entry chamber will be peaceful to walk through since you already vanquished your fear. You can see the stairwell by the light above ground spilling onto the steps. If needed, use the end of the session to chat with your guide in the open field.

For Your Journal

- Which guide (by name or description) leads your way to the entrance? If you received advice or had a conversation as you walked together, write it all down.
- What is the fear-based challenge you encounter upon entering the cavern and how do you overcome it?
- Describe the ritual of the second chamber.
- With whom are you seeking resolution or a greater understanding?
- What transpires in the chamber concerning the proceedings? What guidance do you receive?
- If you discuss the journey with your guide upon exiting, include details of that conversation as well.
- How would you assess your general feeling about the relationship following the meditation as opposed to how it had been prior to this experience? (If you are unsure, you can always come back to journal on this

question in a day or two, once you have had some time to process the information.)

WINDING DOWN:
Meditation to Aid Restful Sleep

Being troubled by restless sleep can be attributed to excess energy in our system, while balanced energy allows us to fall asleep peacefully. This activity meditation is one quick way to manage energy before going to bed.

Begin by going through your usual bedtime routine. You will want the meditation to be the very last thing you do so you can lie down and drift to sleep.

Start the meditation session sitting on the side of your bed with your feet flat on the floor. Put your hands at either side of your legs, resting on the bed, or even holding the edge of it to ensure your balance.

First, spend a minute or two with your eyes closed, listening to your breathing. Notice as it evens out, becoming slower, deeper, and more rhythmic. Inhale fully, relaxing more with each breath. Allow your feet to become heavier, making you feel a sense of groundedness.

Once you are easily concentrating on your breathing, continue with the second part. This begins with letting your head relax and drop forward. Visualize the back of your neck releasing built up energy. You may clairvoyantly see glistening light or a spray of energy as it is discharged. Continue to stretch your spine forward, curving your back as you lean down slowly and gently. Allow your shoulders to relax. Bend only as far as is comfortable for you and no more. Make sure you do not hold your breath. Let your ultra-senses guide you.

Now, sit back up gently. This time start by tipping your head backward. Feel the energy emitted, downward from your face to your neck and throat. Extend the backward stretching motion, arching your back in a relaxed manner. Then, gently sit upright again.

If you find yourself getting dizzy, this is a sign that you have over-extended yourself.

Do this same motion to your left side and repeat it to your right, first tilting your head to the side, then leaning your body to flex your spine. It is a sensation of opening your spinal column to free all energy pockets that are stuck or off-balance.

Once you have stretched all four directions, you are essentially done, but feel free to personalize your method or conclude the relaxation meditation however you wish.

A personal favorite is to stretch your arms straight forward or up until it feels like your very fingertips are made longer, and then again straight out to your sides. Follow this by stretching your toes down and up, then rotating your ankles before lying down. This helps rid of last bits of energy draining out through your extremities. If you lie completely flat, you can do a final, full-body-length stretch before you relax into your sleep position. Whatever leaves you feeling more tranquil, or possibly refreshed and balanced, is going to be helpful.

This is a nice moment to offer up words of gratitude for the day or to say a prayer.

It is further relaxing to lie down and ease into sleep being conscious of your body in a physical sense, then expanding your awareness in a very natural way, until your body feels no separate from the energy of all that surrounds it, so all that is, is completely that...energy.

For those of you who are working on dream studies and interpretation, now would be the moment to set intention or ask that you be able to recall your dreams when you wake up.

A last idea is to bring concentration back to your breathing and fall asleep that way. Whatever it is that you choose to do to customize your routine is perfectly well and good. You will know what works best for you—especially when you wake up after an uninterrupted and peaceful night's sleep.

For Your Journal

- If you are awake and found journaling immediately after doing this meditation, this calls for a do-over, clearly.
- Anything you journal about this meditation the next day should include ideas about what worked the best, or what to try to customize your routine.
- Make a note in your journal of what you were grateful for during the previous day.
- If you are working on dream studies or on connecting in dream-state with your spirit guide, be sure to write these experiences down first thing upon waking, so that you will have a record to refer back to when you need.

RECOVERY

Although meditation, or the information acquired by doing meditation, is in no way a cure or a replacement for traditional medical treatments, possessing greater knowledge of our health does facilitate relief, comfort, or healing on a spiritual level. The most harmonious model for healing integrates traditional, alternative, and spiritual therapies. While this is long understood practice in some parts of the world, Western culture loiters on the cusp.

The intention behind this meditation is to help process illness, whether physical or mental, and to expand comprehension about a situation. Awareness is a vital tool of self-empowerment. When we are ill and feel helpless, a heightened perspective is difficult to muster. That is why such a relaxing resource is so beneficial, and understanding acquired through meditation bolsters us and makes recovery more feasible.

On a personal note, this meditation means a lot to me as my own healing guides originally relayed it to me so that I could give it to a dear friend who was suffering a terrible illness.

The Meditation:
Start by visualizing yourself outdoors, in a very isolated, forested area. There is a dirt walking trail, so you can avoid the overgrowth. A totem animal guide will find you and you can ask it to show you the journey of your illness. Among other things, you may learn about the underlying causes, the purpose it serves, or the effect on

your or others close to you. You may discover information regarding healing, coping, or the recovery process. Follow the animal as it guides you through areas along the path that correspond to various stages of the illness.

By no means do you need to complete the journey in one try or even two. As it can be an energetic challenge to focus at length during illness, visit as many sections as you want to explore at once. For the rest, come back to it another time. You should be able to pick up the trail where you left off. Progress onward until you finish the meditative journey.

Although the word *trail* is used here, realize that you are not required to stay on the starting dirt trail; rather, the *sense* of a trail exists as a constant to ensure you feel safe and not ever lost. As a result, the trail itself may not be all on the ground and it may not always look the same. Flying, skimming across water, floating in space, riding an elephant...let the path take you on your own wondrous adventure.

If you think you have gone off track whatsoever, simply say, "Put me on the trail," and you will immediately be headed in the right direction again. In this same manner, once your totem guide has shown you the entire course, whether in one or multiple sessions, ask to return gently and it will be so.

For Your Journal

◎ Which totem animal came to assist you? Is this a new guide or one with whom you are familiar?

◎ Do you know what healing wisdoms this animal embodies? There may be a message or sign for you in researching that information as well. (See the *Quick-Check Animal Symbolism Guide* on page 270 or use your personal resources).

◎ Record your meditation journey. Be detailed especially about information you collect regarding causes, symptoms, purpose, guidance for healing and recovery, and insights into both traditional and holistic therapies that may aid you.

◎ If impressions of people come to you during the meditation, pay special attention to notating those details, insights, or conversations. They may play a role in your healing. For those who are, as yet, unknown to you, include physical descriptions and other characteristics, in case the person comes into your life later on, then you will have this for reference.

THE PICNIC:
Meditation on Family

What better way to connect with your loved ones than at a family picnic. Coming into this meditation, send out a telepathic invitation, an intention, for all those connected to you in this lifetime, whether in spirit or here, whether you have known them for years or have yet to meet, that they (perhaps as their higher selves) come join you in this meditation to celebrate and deliberate the idea of family.

This meditation can be approached in a few individualized ways, depending on your need, desire, or concern each time. Some ideas include:

- Exploring ways to resolve family conflict to heal wounds or divisions, or to help your family through a challenging situation.
- Setting an intention for learning how to best honor passed loved ones as you move forward in life.
- Using the meditation to bring awareness and clarity about your role within your family, whether in a general sense or alluding to an exact circumstance.
- Gaining an understanding or acceptance of non-traditional, contemporary ideas of family that continue to emerge in society. What is *family* meant to be to you? Who truly composes your family? What are the traditional ties vs. the non-traditional?

The Meditation:

Follow the first "For Your Journal" prompt, setting the intention for your experience, then relax into your usual routine.

Heading out to meet family in this meditation, allow the setting to originate naturally, rather than choosing it. To get your bearings, concentrate on your feet, and when you can see those clearly, let your field of vision expand gradually outward, revealing your location. It may turn out to be a familiar park, a family farm, a resort, or another place you have all reunited before; however, it could be somewhere completely new. Either way, part of the fun in getting there is finding out the location your higher self had in mind for you to see. This can be truly significant if you are meditating with family members in mind who have already passed.

Whichever intention you decided upon as your focus, there will be some meaning as to how you find the others in your meditation in various groupings or seating areas. For this reason, it is important for you to mingle from group to group to see which people comprise each, as well as to find out the literal or symbolic messages within this dynamic. Insights are gained by interacting with the various groups. If you have questions, address them as you go along.

Take into account that the people you see are characterizations for the purpose of the meditation, not the actual people. While you have invited their higher selves, it is not a guarantee that they are participating in a direct way either. The meditation is about you.

Once you have discerned each group, there may be an additional step or task, so watch for this before you return home. This is expected more so if you have set an intention of healing or honoring passed loved ones. All you need to do is ask if anything else is required before you return. There are no conditions set, so this part could present any number of things. For instance, making a symbolic gesture that brings clarity or carrying out a task to promote healing.

It is fine if you feel there is not more to be done. If this is the case, assume that all you needed in the moment was pointed out to you already.

Finish your session by offering an acknowledgment, whether a short thank-you speech to the group in attendance, or by sending general thoughts of gratitude and love toward those people represented at your family picnic. Close your eyes and return as gradually as you need.

At any time, you can repeat this meditation to use it for whichever of the different purposes, or for an idea of your own. If you do revisit to gain further details on the same topic, it is probable you will find yourself at the same location. Though, if you try the meditation with a new intention, hold back expectation. The setting is sure to change, as are the dynamics of people newly represented.

For Your Journal

- ◎ What purpose did you choose for the meditation this time? Take a few minutes to journal the situation, challenge, or your current feelings on the matter before going into the meditation. Do you have any presumed ideas about *family* before you begin?
- ◎ What setting reveals itself to you for your family picnic? What were your first impressions of it?

◎ Which people did you first notice? Were there other significant details that quickly piqued your interest?

◎ Describe the process of mingling with the various groups of family. How many groupings did you discover and who comprises each? What connection or purpose lies between them? Are there emotional or physical elements that are important to notice?

◎ What concepts, insights, or understanding do you arrive at by going from group to group?

◎ Do certain groups or people surprise you or bring awareness of an unexpected aspect of family?

◎ Are there groups or individuals for whom you find more compassion or ease of understanding?

◎ Translate symbolic messages received, as you are able. Leave space if needed to come back to it later.

◎ Is there an extra step before completing the meditation? If so, what does this entail? What is the purpose or meaning behind it? What do you feel this will allow you (e.g., an extra level of faith, confidence, resolution, healing, or assurance)?

Side Note on the Family Meditation:

Though all the meditations in this book technically may be done in a group setting, this meditation has a very personal theme, and for that reason, may trigger heightened emotional responses. This is generally one of those meditations best done on your own, in private. At the very least, if you do this meditation with others present, give the participants the choice to opt out and make them aware of the possibilities of surfacing emotions before they begin. In all fairness, this is the best way to respect and protect everyone's privacy.

🦋 Regarding Kindred Mates, Kindred Spirits, and Soul Mates

When you are trying to manifest new and better aspects in your life by using meditation, affirmation, or other means, knowing exactly what you are searching for is essential. This truly applies when it comes to the idea of looking for a love relationship. History, culture, and fiction teach us to search for our soul mates in life. My spirit guides had a few words for me on this topic, so the best way to explain is to share with you what they told me:

"It is not your *soul* mate you are looking for; it is your *kindred* mate."

There is a difference? Apparently so. As my guides went on to explain, the soul mates we relentlessly seek in life, the ones we identify with the idea of pure and unconditional love, are not actually here. Our true soul mates generally do not incarnate with us, but rather they tend to remain on the other side, watching over us, and waiting when we return *Home*. As with most all life matters, there are rare exceptions to this of course, where a soul mate acts as a special spirit guide, appears here for a brief but necessary event, or lives for a temporarily overlapping period.

Kindred spirits we encounter regularly in a lifetime. These are the people we are drawn to, regardless of gender, age, race, location, or romantic preferences, who we have an unmistakable familiarity with upon meeting. They unexpectedly turn up in our lives and with a brief conversation have us feeling we have known them forever. They are those remarkable bonds and inexplicable connections our soul and higher self recognizes when they come along, whether it is for a brief interaction or for a great duration of our life.

Iyanla Vanzant, author and inspirational speaker, coined the phrase that I love best to clarify the time we are with another, "for a reason, a season, or a lifetime." Sometimes our soul agreements are met in a moment; sometimes it is about fulfilling a purpose or helping one another get through an impactful time in life. Other times, a most rare blessing occurs—finding a relationship to last a lifetime. This is not a justification to treat people that come into our lives flippantly, or to view our relationships as expendable. Instead, it is a call to be decidedly thoughtful and wise to our interactions, for every person we encounter in life, is there for, at minimum, a reason.

The people we truly are seeking here for our love relationships then are our *kindred mates*. They are the people we choose as intimate connections, our marriage partners, our long-term loves. They may not be immediately familiar and recognizable to us as a kindred spirit, as we may or may not have lifetimes of history with them, but Divine timing tends to expose the true nature of the connection.

After speaking at a high school one afternoon, a student approached me to explain that he was going to be graduating and would be heading straight into the military. His concern was about parting from his then girlfriend, as her path would be taking her in a completely different direction. They were clearly struggling with a looming and unavoidable breakup. He wanted to know if we have a solitary chance at true love, one soul mate. Whether 18-years-old or 68, we may face this human turmoil. Because, even when we believe we have found a kindred mate, this relationship, too, could be for a short-lived "season."

Unforeseeable circumstances, differences in life paths, completed soul agreements. Countless incidents could pull us apart in an instant, so whenever you are fortunate enough to have time with one of these special people, make the most of the days that you do have together and remember to honor it. Love wholly. Listen. Share. Make sacrifices and compromises. Apologize and forgive. Build a foundation of absolute respect. Be mindful and conscious of your gratitude for what that person brings to your life.

Then, if life should divide you, know it is possible to continue to love those who are not present. Sometimes that means allowing a loved one the freedom to continue on a separate life path. Sometimes we are not given a choice and they are taken from us. No matter the circumstances, we honor our self and the other by understanding that when we do leave this lifetime, we will again be together. We will then be privy to all the "why's and what for's."

Auspiciously for us and for that student, there is not a lone kindred mate we have written into our life plan. That would truly amount to lives spent searching for a single prince in world of imposters. So, if you have lost a love, be hopeful and watchful, the next significant person in your life, whether kindred spirit or kindred mate, could be a few steps away. That is part of what keeps life exciting.

ATTRACTING a LOVE

Initially, as you listen to your breathing, briefly think about where love grows from in your life. This will inspire the opening setting for your meditation. From there, position yourself to be outdoors. Notice the small hill ahead in the distance. Despite its apparent ordinariness, by standing at the top you are able to see for miles around you. Hold your hands up to your heart chakra for a moment. Then, cup your hands moving them outward. A brilliant sphere of light in a shade of green or pink, or a swirl of both, fills your hands. Extend your hands forward, thinking of your intentions for this beacon of light.

What is it about love that you want to invite toward you? State a simple affirmation regarding your intent and desire, such as, "I open my heart to you, my kindred mate, and I am ready for you to be a part of my life." At that point, raise your hands until this powerful light begins to float upward to a position out of reach above you. Watch as it grows brighter, then suddenly expands, causing a ripple effect of light to wash outward and away from you. The loving energy of the Universe guides it to move as far as it need go to reach this special person. Let the light energy go freely and have faith that Divine timing will do the rest.

Wait until you see the wave of ripples returning to you before you return down the hill. Feel the sense of peace, confidence, and joy that washes over you, realizing you have connected with your beloved.

In the weeks or months following, regard it as a time of preparation for welcoming new love into your life. Focus on your own needs and interests; the more you grow, the more interesting you become. Create balance and warmth. Nest. When the relationship arrives, you will have so much to offer and will be ready for what joys come next.

For Your Journal

◎ Where did your meditation begin? (Frequently, this represents a place of comfort or safety). The opening scene and going to the outdoor overlook is symbolic of moving from your comfort zone, to a place of new, unfettered perspective.

◎ Describe the panoramic view from atop the hill, especially, with respect to perspective and natural or man-made features that appear with clarity. Take into account their symbolic or literal interpretations.

◎ What color was the sphere of light you brought forth? Refer to the *Color Guide* (page 267) for further insights.

◎ Write down the intention or affirmation you used in the meditation. Continue to use the affirmation on a regular basis.

◎ For some people, as the wave of light pings off your beloved, the ripples that come back to you may unintentionally yield impressions or insights about the person. Anticipate that it would be fuzzy and incomplete, but be sure to journal it. Validation needed to understand the experience will come eventually.

◎ Another time, think about adapting the meditation for inviting new friendships and kindred spirits, too.

A SYMBOL of HOPE:
Meditation for Luck

"Luck is when preparation meets opportunity."
-Seneca

Before you begin this meditation, evaluate your opinion of *luck*. To do so, mull over and do a little journaling using the following questions as they relate to your focal concern for the meditation. What are your thoughts on luck in general? Are you having "bad luck" or is it a matter of unpreparedness? Are you passing up opportunities or are they not arriving yet? Is apparent unluckiness instead a struggle with patience? It can be trying to wait on Divine timing. Do you feel like your efforts all come to a standstill? Perhaps your higher self, your spirit guide, or the Universe is trying to show you other options. What feels like "bad luck" is sometimes an express result of trying to force or control an issue.

It is important to define your questions on the situation that is troubling you. This will set the intention for your questions to be answered during the meditation. Consider what knowledge you want to gain. Is the Universe trying to direct you to a new course? Is there more you could do? Are there extra facets of which you have been unaware? Is there a way to exchange control for faith to allow Divine timing to work? Is the "bad luck" only a misperception of events in life trying to align a better future for you? Is there a clue to watch for that will bring clearer understanding?

Most of the time, encountering feelings of bad luck and misfortune are indicative of a complex situation at hand. It tends to be less about *luck*, and more about our own resistance or willingness to change. Our refusal to leave a comfort zone or belligerence in recognizing the responsibility that we have to our life purpose holds us back. We find it easy to be accepting when circumstances flow smoothly, less so when we are faced with change, transformation, and crossroads.

How can we be more open to the process, so we can once again feel life is bringing us forward with *good* luck? Moments like this definitely call for the wisdom and knowledge of a higher power. (I feel like we are about to beckon the newest Avenger superhero, so if your higher self or spirit guide appears in your meditation donning brightly colored Lycra and Spandex, my advance apologies. Then again, they do know best when we need to lighten up or could use a laugh, so if they do, all the more blessings for us).

The Meditation:

Let your list of questions suggest your starting setting. In that way, it will be symbolic of where your "bad luck" appears to originate. With that in mind, you might imagine yourself at work if your career is in crisis, or at home if your relationship (or lack of one) is in shambles. You could even see yourself sitting in your car if it is in need of repairs.

As you imagine this place, take an observational position. Let your vision follow a line of thought to complete an accurate picture for you as to the true nature of the matter. Perhaps you see a scene unfold that provides broader understanding, or you become aware of under-lying currents of which you had no prior knowledge. You may see past events replayed alluding to the root of the problem.

It is also possible that representations of people appear in your meditation, if you feel your luck is associated with another person who has influence over your life. Someone may speak to explain information to you. Try to be open and reserve judgment and defensiveness. Hold questions until this part of the meditation is complete by keeping a removed position.

There is a chance of whisking away to a new setting as your awareness shifts, so allow time for the imagery to become clear before you proceed. Once you feel the true perspective is evident, speak with a guide regarding how to best proceed. Use that opportunity to ask specific questions from your prepared list. Examples follow: Is a certain course of action in your best interest? Will a specific person be able to help you through this period? What improves your drive, inspiration, and positivity? Is there a change or transition taking place and are there significant factors to be aware of currently? Is there anything you ought to take action on to alter your luck? Would it serve you best to be patient or to redirect your efforts elsewhere for the time being?

At the end of this second part of the meditation, search the space you find yourself in at that moment, looking for a symbol of hope and good luck to take back with you. After you find this, thank guides who have helped you along the way and then return home.

For Your Journal

- For the pre-meditation exercise on "luck," write down your thoughts and answers to the relevant questions that were posed.
- Whether you prepared one question or a list to address in your meditation, include that in your journal entry, along with space to detail insights you receive as a result.
- What setting did you decide upon to visualize as your starting point for the meditation?
- What is taking place in your life that brought you to that choice?
- Did a certain guide or your higher self assist you in the meditation?
- What circumstances are underlying your misfortune or "bad luck"?
- Describe the true perspective you are shown.
- Record other questions addressed along with the replies.
- What more should you do to prepare, so you will be ready when the opportunity presents itself?
- What advice do you receive about how to feel lucky again? What role does gratitude play in this?
- Sketch or describe the symbol of hope, your good luck charm, which you find.

Post-Meditation:

As a follow-up activity, breathe physical-world life into your lucky charm by re-creating it somehow. Carve the piece from wood, draw or paint it, mold it out of clay, wood burn the symbol on a small cutout...whatever you are inspired to do. Whenever you see your lucky charm, it will bring you that same positive perspective of hope and affirmation as when you discover it in your meditation.

LAKSHMI'S TEMPLE:
Meditation for Abundance & Prosperity

What does abundance mean to you? The truth is that abundance reveals itself in a variance of ways throughout a person's lifetime. What you viewed as abundance ten years ago may no longer be the same as your ideal picture of that today. The real key to feeling life is abundant, is that it happens when life is unquestionably balanced. It is not about measurement, haves or have-nots. It most certainly has nothing to do with the Joneses. It is about peace. When balance comes, you recognize harmony in your well-being, family, career, friendships, spiritual life, and other elements. You may think of them as successful or perhaps even prosperous. Unquestionably, this does not mean that everything must be perfect and that you have no challenges, bad days, struggles, or sacrifices to make. What it *does* mean is that even when one aspect is waning, another aspect of your life is supporting, blossoming, or alleviating the first, in a way that you can see how the aspects of your life are working together with symmetry.

As an example, perhaps you are going through a bout with illness, but at the same time, you find that suddenly a family member or friend you had been out of touch with arrives to support you through your healing. You can probably think of events going on right now where similar ebb and flow is apparent. When aspects of your life come together in this harmonious way of filling gaps or supporting another, your life is working in an abundant manner. Now and then, it can be hard to see past the lacking aspects to recognize those that are in excess, at least until it is all in hindsight, but if you do take account, you will see this on some level.

In a circumstance of feeling unbalance or "more ebbing than flowing," meditation is one activity you can trust to bring insight, new perspective, and guidance, so as to improve awareness of what is happening. Learn if there are blocks you are manifesting and if an action can rectify this. It is feasible to open yourself to a higher level of abundance and prosperity than you have been experiencing to this point.

People call upon Hindu goddess of good fortune, Lakshmi, and her counterpart, Ganesh, god of prosperity and wisdom, as ascended masters, in energy or presence, to offer guidance in times of need. One or both are able to show us from where our difficulties spring, how we are preventing progress toward personal abundance, or even how our perceptions are misconstrued.

The Meditation:

Outside a lush green area, your meditative sight sharpens into focus on exotic surroundings. Nearby, there is an entryway, archway, or gate. Walking through this leads you to a remarkable, open-air style spiritual center or temple with a nurturing, inviting feel. As a guest, you are welcome to wander around until you find a place that best suits your mood. Sit comfortably where you can concentrate and observe. Choose from one of the many nooks—sheltered alcoves, benches below trees, and peaceful plots of grass among tall flowers. When you have selected precisely the right spot, decide on a central question about abundance. Listed are several ideas to use as a guide for drawing your own line of thought, either on a personal level or on a wider scale:

- Though I feel certain aspects of my life are filled with abundance, I always feel that my _____ (finances, friendships, health, living arrangement, romantic life, etc.) are constantly a struggle. I would like to better understand myself and how to overcome my personal challenges, so that I experience true prosperity and happiness.

- I am unsure of how to create abundance in my life. Where are my blockages to this and how do I remove them, so I can open my path to all of life's blessings...to fulfill my potential?

- Please show me how to balance aspects of my life so I can find peace and true happiness through abundance.

- I feel like I have abundance in these aspects of my life: _____, _____, _____, yet I still do not feel the level of happiness I anticipated would accompany this abundance. Please help me to understand this and guide me to improve my situation.

- What role do I play in helping or hindering the prosperity of _____(my family, my community, the company I work for, etc.)?

- How can I help others find their way to abundance and prosperity, much as I experience it in my own life?

- As human beings, how does prosperity influence our happiness or other aspects of life on Earth?

As you meditate in your nook, others may join you to speak to you, or you may make an observation that helps to answer your question. Alternately, you may receive sincere guidance communicated through direct, ultra-sensory messages and awareness. Be open to all the possibilities as they come to you.

Before you return, you will find (or be given) a gold coin. When this happens, shift toward expressions of gratitude, whether that be one small idea, or a list you have been storing up for a while that begins to pour out of you. See, feel, and know that your thoughts are going out into the Universe, every time you express gratefulness. This beautiful energy will be magnified and cause a ripple effect of grace and beauty coming back into your life, too. Use one of the following affirmations or create one of your own to confirm your new understanding. (See *How to Write an Affirmation*, page 236).

- ⊚ Through gratitude, my life is abundant and filled with happiness.
- ⊚ As a loving being of Light, I am at peace and I open myself to receiving all the blessings of the world.
- ⊚ As I achieve balance of my spirituality, wisdom, and gratitude, I find true abundance, happiness, and peace.

Keep the coin from your meditation with you as you return through the entryway, as a symbol of this cycle of gratitude and abundance. See how it manifests and multiplies in your life, and be filled with joy and happiness.

May blessings of abundance be yours, today and always!

For Your Journal

- Detail your account of the outer parts of the temple or spiritual center. How did you find the entryway to be?
- What were the various sitting places once you were within the temple? How did you arrive at the nook you chose to sit in? What were its unique features? What drew you to it?
- What was the principal question you chose?
- Explain the guidance you received and how that came to you.
- Were there symbolic aspects to your experience?
- Did you notice any repetition of aspects within the temple? (White lotus flowers and elephants are symbols often surrounding Lakshmi and Ganesh.)
- How did you come across your coin? Do you see a literal or symbolic parallel between that and the possibilities of how you discover abundance in your life?
- Write down the expression of gratitude you used in your meditation, as well as your affirmation. Carry your affirmation with you on a small piece of paper for the days to follow as a reminder of the intentions you have set. A little Post-It note put somewhere you will see it each day works, too.

AN ANGEL'S GUIDANCE:
Meditation for Recognizing Your Gifts

When we feel stuck, uncertain, or fearful of how to proceed in life it is not always a question of unwillingness or being closed-off to change. The obstacle we face may be the simpler matter of not recognizing what our true gifts are. Without this understanding, how can we possibly anticipate what type of opportunities might arrive? We go in circles thinking, "That can't possibly be for me," "I don't know how to...," "I've never done...," "I'm not sure if...." Thoughts like those consistently get in our way. Worse still, we create narrow limitations because change can be scary. We allow outgrown and outmoded elements of our past or from our comfort zone, to be our deciding factors, even if it means repeating a cycle we know did not work for us before.

If we have dreams that have not yet come to fruition, or if we have prayed for change, however, it is important to recognize opportunity when it comes. Is it time to move on to a completely new endeavor, even if it is bewildering? We are not marooned on one lot in life. Varied jobs on a lengthy résumé are the building blocks for a future career. Failed relationships are a foundation for the wisdom necessary to cultivate a healthy, long-term relationship. Logic and rational analysis oftentimes get in our way because it feels safer to choose what you already know. Unfortunately, that does not allow for emerging gifts, divinely timed chances, opportune meetings, or all those other unknown factors and unexpected variables life is ready to surprise us with.

In this case, Archangel Chamuel can be of the greatest assistance to us. By calling upon him in thought or meditation, he will help us recognize our true gifts. *Gifts* being those characteristics, natural abilities, or learned skills that we carry in this lifetime for the intention of fulfilling our soul agreements and life purpose. It is sometimes hard for us to see that which is so ingrained in us, or to recognize a normal part of ourselves as distinctive or special, yet these are the parts of us in this human lifetime that we are meant to share with others. These strengths are our gifts.

Have you ever asked your friends what they perceive to be your best qualities? They often point out strengths that you did not recognize in yourself, or aspects that you took for granted. Connecting with Archangel Chamuel is like this, at an exponentially higher level of understanding and accuracy. He offers us guidance to point us in the right direction with work-related abilities, as well as those we apply to relationships. Archangel Chamuel knows our soul's plan and brings needed comfort, signs, messages, or reassurance.

The Meditation:

To begin your meditation, use the following invocation, filling in the blanks to suit your personal need or issue.

> *I call upon you, Archangel Chamuel, to help me recognize my true gifts and how they affect my _____ (life purpose, relationships, career, hobby, marriage, friendship, etc.). Please guide me through this meditation so I will see my true self and be able to emerge with a refreshed*

sense of_____ (hope, confidence, inspiration, under-standing, etc.). Let me know, too, what symbolic sign to watch for in the days ahead so I will be able to maintain this sense of purpose as I go on.

Starting out, as your surroundings become clear, you will notice the boxed-in aspect of your environment. It could be a square room, a high-fenced enclosure outdoors, or any number of similar places representative of the comfort zone you have constructed for yourself over time. Because what surrounds you is symbolic of what is familiar and safe to you, this place should not bear a sense of negativity or worry, aside from the possibility you sense that you want it to change or expand in some way.

Go around the entire perimeter of the space. Stop at each opening, window, doorway, passage, or gate. Look to see how these appear, noticing which are currently open or closed, and more importantly, noticing the labels on every one of these openings. These are illustrative pieces of your character, your strengths, and your gifts. Take into consid-eration those facets which have been there a long while, or those you have always been aware of, compared to those that are a surprise to you, or those qualities of yourself that you have not considered previously.

Through this process, recognition comes about how strengths and gifts have already served your life path. You may even have flashbacks to events in your lifetime, perhaps to moments long forgotten. Claircognizant im-pressions expose correlation between events and purpose; links that you never discerned may suddenly become clear. Be accepting of the revelations necessary to you.

Notice then, the fully or partially closed openings. You can go back to one or more that you are intrigued by, or that you strongly feel urged to study. In doing this, ask the assistance of Archangel Chamuel, that the quality or gift signified be made open and available to you should it be in your best interest or serve a true purpose. If further action or process is required on your part, it will be made clear to you.

During the entirety of the meditation, should it be important to see beyond the boxy perimeter through one of the openings, feel free to do so, but be sure you return to that starting square in every instance.

Spend as much time here as you wish. You may communicate with your higher self, your spirit guide, or with Archangel Chamuel, so if you find you need more clarity, ask open questions before you finish. Sometimes the answers are revealed in ways we do not expect, and sometimes outside the time frame we wish, so assume if you do not sense the answers immediately, that they will be forthcoming, in most Divinely timed ways.

Do not forget to retrieve or ask for your "sign" before you finish, as it will be a helpful validation in the days following your meditation.

For Your Journal

◎ In bringing gifts to light, which topic or aspect did you settle on when you called upon Archangel Chamuel?

◎ Describe the square environment in which your meditation takes place. Include notes especially regarding the openings, their labels, and which are open, closed, or partially accessible.

◎ Journal insights that have surfaced about events in your past or present. It is a good idea to leave space to come back later in the week to add further thoughts, as important memories may now be unlocked and could emerge in the days following your meditation.

◎ Did you explore out beyond one of the passages? If so, what did the passage represent or how was it labeled? What do you feel was the necessity for doing so? What would you have missed if you had bypassed that step?

◎ Which openings, closed or partially so, did you decide to adjust, or, did you opt to leave everything as-is? What was the process in doing this?

◎ Concerning newly opened passages, how do you feel you might best manifest or apply the associated gifts and abilities in the short term? What are your thoughts on how they could help you with long-term aspects of your life? Are there specific people you already know who may benefit from you sharing your gifts?

◎ Make a note of the sign and its symbolism. After the meditation, should it turn up, write about the significance and timing of those occurrences, and the validation that you receive.

Post-Meditation:

It complements your meditation work to write an affirmation that you can use daily to assist you in accessing, manifesting, and realizing all your gifts. As new situations come up in your life, you will want to add journal entries, so at some time in the future you will have this to look back on. It will encapsulate your hard work and how far you have come.

How to Write an Affirmation

The Power of Affirmations

A true affirmation is a precise declaration. You declare what you believe, desire, or imagine your life to be, with the intention being to draw this aspect into your life. The objective is to manifest aspects into becoming a reality.

Our actions, words, and thoughts are the constructive tools for us to apply our gift of free will in life. We are not required to use them haphazardly, unconsciously. They are all *living* energy. For example, when confronted with a challenge. If we are uncertain about our ability and we say, "I can't do that," we cannot. We have made it so by setting the limitation. If instead we say, "I will give it a try," despite our uncertainty, the possibilities remain open. We leave the potential to complete the challenge up to our active effort in trying. What we think, say, or do, all works in accordance, thereby bringing aspects of life into being.

The task of writing and thoughtfully making up affirmations is an easy way to create, contemplatively and deliberately, facets of our lives, instead of leaving everything to unmindful and arbitrary human response.

Using affirmations with regularity helps us to positively modify our thoughts, working as a creative means to evoke change in our lives. It is a way to more propitious experiences and greater fulfillment. When you create a positive thought through an affirmation, you are sending that constructive, active energy into the Universe. You are, in effect, manifesting your reality.

Guidelines for Writing Affirmations

◉ Keep the affirmation short and simple. It will be easier to remember, and you will be more inclined to use it.

◉ Write in active present tense. I know, I am, I have, I see, I open to, I do, I succeed, I experience, I love.

◉ Do not use the verbs "want," "wish," or "hope." To do so creates the want, wish, or hope; it creates a *potential*, but not what you are seeking. Likewise, do not use the word "will," as it sets the intention in the future. Ultimately, to use one of these keeps your desired outcome at a distance, unable to manifest itself.

◉ Choose your words thoughtfully, carefully, and specifically. You have heard the saying, "Be careful what you wish for, you may get it." If you are vague, the response to your affirmation may be vague. If your thoughts are specific, but you do not put this into your affirmation, then what you truly had in mind may not come to pass.

◉ Construct affirmations from a position of love, not fear.

◉ Keep your affirmation somewhere you see it, some place it reminds you to say it or read it once or twice every day.

◉ Remember, affirmations are a practical way to work with creative energy. It is one segment of the energetic process and many other factors apply, such as faith, responsibility, expectation, Divine timing, and integrity to name a few. Do not set conditions or you will limit yourself and the possibilities for the fulfillment of the affirmation.

This brings me to the most useful affirmation. Use it as often as needed. Whenever facing doubt and confusion, or when life gives the impression that it is going awry, it can help put things back into perspective and bring our mindset of calm and faith back to us. The affirmation is simply this: "I trust my path."

The affirmations you choose are personal, so you are encouraged to write your own, in your own words. Here are a few examples to get you started:

- I have faith.
- I know that I am loved.
- I am confident and inspired.
- Today I am perfect exactly as I am.
- Supportive family and friends fill my life.
- I open myself to my spiritual whole.
- I feel blessed with good health and balance in life.
- Abundance comes easily to me. I have all I need.
- The answers I seek are clear.
- I have a fulfilling job that aligns to my life purpose.
- I see the beauty in the little things today.
- I clearly see the choices that are in my best interest.
- I note the best opportunity and am prepared to act.
- I am part of the cycle of giving and receiving; what I lovingly put forth always comes back.
- I am willing.
- I have patience.
- I trust *their* path.

OUTPOURING:
Meditation for Calming Energy

This meditation is best used when feeling a sense of anxiety, nervousness, or agitation. It is a meditation my healing guide conveyed to me, for a client who was suffering panic attacks. It was ideal because she could use the meditation as a complement to her traditional medical care. In no way is this singular meditation, or any other, a cure or substitution for traditional therapies, or an alternative for working with physical and mental health practitioners. A person does not need to be suffering extremely for this meditation to be useful, but it is an empowering tool in many circumstances.

My healing guide described it to me saying that if a person uses this meditation at the very instant of anxiety beginning to build, the person regains focus and an active sense of choice and control. This is a practical method to aid understanding and management of one's own energy. It works by moving awareness of one's own energy away from its inward effects, transferring it outwardly to a creational opportunity of positivity, balance, and giving. What could otherwise transpire into very upsetting circumstance shifts into an opportunity of grace.

One of the best things about this meditation is that once familiar with how it works, you can do it wherever or whenever you need. Eyes closed or eyes open, very quickly, or quite slowly with more thought put into the process. It is also not terribly complex; both adults and children alike have been able to use and benefit from it.

The Meditation:

During this meditation, the key is to become sensitive and attuned to your own body and to the energy flowing through your system. The setting is secondary, and you need not even alter it from where you are sitting, though if your environment is playing a role in your stress levels, you can quite easily visualize yourself in a neutral, safe, or peaceful setting instead. Whatever that is to you, personally—a lush garden, a secluded beach, or a quiet rooftop in the city—is completely fine.

Your main task is to try to draw all your senses inward to your own body. Apply your ultra-senses to see and feel the energy entering your system, watching as it flows in through the top of your head. Maintain steady, rhythmic breathing. Physically extend your arms in front of you comfortably with your hands held open, apart a slight distance as if holding a softball or grapefruit. Feel the energy that is in excess, pull that through your arms, downward, and out into your hands. Allow it to circulate freely, not depleting your own energy, but rather balancing it by drawing the excess outside your system, weaving itself around to create a ball of energy. As the excess streams out, feel this energy increase in size so that your hands move apart to hold what is more the size of a soccer ball. As this occurs, sense the disconnection from the anxiety as the excess energy leaves your system.

When your ball of light and energy feels complete to you, ask of God, your angels, your healing guides, or the Universe, to now send away this excess energy, which was causing you difficulties, to someone who is in need of more, so it may be used in a positive way. Doing so brings healing and balance to you both. Send the energy forth with unconditional love and positive intentions. Allow it to float away, throw it hard, or toss it up and watch it explode into incandescent shards, as it travels to the one in need. This could be someone you are acquainted with or a complete stranger. Given unconditionally, to whom the energy goes is not important. Instead, in the instant the energy moves away from you, try to remain, receptive and quiet. You may be able to glimpse a moment of oneness...your connection to the Divine, and to the remarkable sense of peace and fulfillment that lingers with that healing experience.

For Your Journal

◎ Although this meditation is quite freestanding, if you do journal your experiences, make note of what worked best about the process or if anything hindered it. That way with subsequent sessions, you can make small personal alterations to find the best formula for yourself.

◎ If you chose a special setting for your meditation, write about the place you chose or discovered. How was it a source of calming and peacefulness or of grounding to you?

NO WORRIES
Rosemary

The meditation is elegantly simple and accessible. It activates my ultra-senses and bypasses my mental chatter. This invites my observer-self to the table. When I was first getting familiar with the meditation, I chose a secluded spot. Since then, I have used this meditation when I am standing in the grocery store line. I tried it when the customer ahead of me was coughing and blowing her nose. Usually, I get worried that I will catch the person's cold. I also tried this several times when I heard sirens and when there were cars sliding into the ditches during icy weather. I did this meditation when I was outside ice-skating. It was very nice. I will use this meditation when I am gardening in warmer weather.

Often, I wake up in the middle of the night worried about family members. The Outpouring *meditation is something very tangible that I can do whenever I am worried. I feel grateful that I know how to do this now.*

ROUNDABOUT

Paths and roads give us reassurance as they guide us. It is only a matter of time before they bring us to new adventures, to loved ones, to home. What our soul most yearns for is ahead if we trust our path to lead us there.

Everyone needs a little insight from time to time when it comes to finding your way in life. This meditation aims to help with precisely that. Whether feeling stuck, at a crossroads, or plainly stagnant, the following meditative journey provides answer, clues, and advice to get you feeling back on track. It is helpful regarding relationships, jobs, life purpose, or in general instances of needing a boost or nudge.

The Meditation:

As you ease into your meditation, you find yourself at a deserted city street intersection or a roundabout. Let the scene become clear enough to get your bearings, so you can view the whole area if you rotate 360°. Notice street signs, shop or business names, and other features that stand out to you. Proceed to walk around and explore one of the directions. You may turn back at any point to choose another avenue to investigate. As you advance through the meditation, take notice of the differences on each route. The road behind you as you began should feel familiar, with characteristics and symbols that have brought you to the present. The routes to the front and sides of you should give indication of other possibilities, clues to new opportunities, or aspects of events unfolding. Consider all the options, all the symbolism. Look at the structures and their condition, the shop fronts and window displays, the streets, signage, and other objects dotting the way.

Are you seeing prominent elements that were missing from your originating direction on other avenues?

Find the answers and messages you need right now in all of these things. Allow your claircognizance to work to bring you clarity and peace of mind through greater understanding. Use this part of the session for exploring, then when you are ready to come back, return to the center of the intersection or roundabout. Face in the direction you are compelled to travel ahead on as you close your eyes on the scene and allow your consciousness to return home.

Fill in the last word of this affirmation to use it in closing or write another of your own:

"From this moment forward I am open and aware to the signs and synchronicities around me that will help me proceed in the direction I must go. I am _____! (blessed, at peace, happy, confident, etc)."

For Your Journal

◎ As the focus of this meditation, what is your main concern or the life topic you are feeling is at a standstill?

◎ Record the story of your meditation, being especially careful to note significant detail in the order you encountered each aspect. (There may be meaning for you behind the sequence).

◎ Describe the routes in five words. What are the greatest differences or commonalities between the routes that you perceived?

◎ Write down the affirmation as you used it in closing your meditation session. Keep the affirmation on a note in your pocket or posted where you alone can see it, as a reminder to continue using it for a while. Alternatively, every day you could use the final phrase of the affirmation as a re-affirmation of your chosen direction.

THE BLESSINGS of NOW
Sarah

Throughout the last couple of years, I have prayed so hard for a harmonious marriage. When I practiced this meditation, I was looking from side to side at each option on the roundabout and I saw very clearly and experienced alternative options for my life. Different spouses, different kids, and an entirely different life. I experienced each of those to some extent. Then, I decided to go straight through the roundabout and came to my present life, my marriage, my kids, and I was filled with extreme joy, happiness, light, and what felt like immeasurably great blessings. For a moment, I felt as if it was heaven, but it was my life. It has brought me immense joy to feel and experience all my current life experiences with these vast blessings. This meditation brought me such happiness with this life.

MANDORLA MEDITATION

There is a name for the almond-shape created by two intersecting or overlapping circles. It is called a *mandorla*.

Circles have always been a representation of the limitless and unending. Wedding rings, prayer circles, dream catchers, labyrinths–all meaningful and strongly symbolic variations of this shape. Think, then, of the energetic and symbolic possibilities of uniting two of these circles. Mandorlas have the power to heal, to transform, to reconcile, to enlighten, and to bring complete under-standing of a truth. Imagine two opposing forces, or two conflicting perspectives. If you view those as individual circles that then overlap or collide into one another, you have a mandorla. Within that common space, those two opposites that have been in a state of disharmony or misunderstanding, can find resolve. A mandorla is a bridge uniting two varied, freestanding viewpoints, opinions, or ways, and it is always filled with hope.

The versatile mandorla meditation has four different purposes, so before you begin, select the one you would like to apply.

1. **Cycles**: To learn how to break free from a recurring cycle in your life.

For this option, first decide on what the pattern and outcome, or the cause and reaction tend to be in the cycle. Then, note what you consider the ideal or what the best possible alternative to the cycle would be. Each of these will comprise one circle of the mandorla in your meditation. Think, "how it is" vs. "how you desire it to be."

2. **Differences:** To find the truth or common ground of a life issue or a relationship disparity.

Using the meditation in this way, you will need to define two separate components. This may be two people's names, or it could be the two possibilities, opinions, viewpoints, or theories involved. If you have these two labels loosely defined before starting the meditation it will be a more fluid process. The circles indicate either "the first aspect" vs. "the second aspect," or each person.

3. **Decisions:** To gain information necessary to make a decision when there are two choices.

When meditating for help with a decision, take a minute to clarify the two choices. Assign a word or short phrase to label each. You can use the meditation to find pros and cons to the options. Try to discover if there is a way to merge or compromise the two choices. The two circles symbolize the two choices.

4. **Understanding:** To better understand your connection to another person.

All you need to begin with this meditation are your two names. The circles each represent one of you.

The Meditation:

The walkway you discover at the start of this meditation will lead you into a grand, expansive courtyard. View your spectacular surroundings in this place of enlightenment. Whether you discover ornate buildings, lush foliage, artistic sculptures, or something else, you will feel the peacefulness and know that you are protected, safe, and healed by being here.

Toward the center of the courtyard is a more open space. As you approach this area, you will find a very simple pattern manifesting itself on the ground as two interlocking circles. Much like labyrinths, the looping design appears as a path, perhaps of garden paving blocks, stone, bricks, gravel, wood shavings, or a freshly mowed track.

Walk the outline of the first circle, and then go into the center where you can label it in some way. Repeat this for the second circle. This sets the intention for what each circle represents. If you are limited for time, you can bypass walking the path of the circles and directly enter the centers to mark each intention.

Once each circle is defined, enter into the almond-shaped mandorla. You will find there is a spot to sit comfortably. While there, listen in a state of relaxed consciousness to the messages awaiting you. Consider all you hear, see, and feel as you are engaged in this open level of awareness. Sometimes a message will not be in words, but rather arrives as a vision or scene. Perhaps even the sensations or emotions experienced during the meditation present an answer. Try not to jump to questions or analysis as information begins to flow through. Instead, take a more observational position so you do not stop the process.

When you sense a natural break or a pause in the insights, then go ahead to ask clarifying questions to get details, especially if an aspect is symbolic rather than literal, or if there is slight confusion on your part. Remember though, once you have asked a question you will need to return to that perfectly open state of calm to best receive the replies. Stay in this mandorla until you feel ready to return.

With your allotted meditation time, you can opt to exit the mandorla straightaway offering an expression or token of gratitude, then departing the courtyard and stepping back onto the walkway, or you can leisurely exit by walking the circles in reverse order. If you opt for this more gradual return, you will see the circles dissipate behind you, with the central mandorla still visible as you exit the courtyard, following the walkway back home.

Group Variation:

For an even-numbered group of people, divide into pairs for the meditation. The partners then use the session to discover more about their personal ties to each other. It is a fun exercise in the understanding of oneness and universal connection.

If you opt to do this meditation together, it is a more symbolic gesture if the participants bring along two of their own open-circle objects to hold onto during the meditation. Once everyone pairs off, trade the circle objects so each person will hold one of her own items along with one of her partner's. The objects need not be of a set, or even matching whatsoever. They could be jewelry; rings and earrings work well. Key rings, steel washers, canning lids, a small embroidery hoop, or a ponytail holder, are just a few other suggestions. Anything that is a circle with an open center should work.

When the circles manifest in the courtyard ground, pay special attention to see how the two personalized circles reveal themselves as pathways to walk, as it may be unique to the occasion.

Following the meditation and time allowed for journaling, initiate a group discussion on the topic of oneness, talking about how we are all interconnected. It is a good way to weave everyone's practical, daily life experiences together with the group's shared experiences and meditation stories.

For Your Journal

- Which of the four options did you choose? What were the two separate aspects for this session?
- Describe your courtyard, noting especially the unique features, a characteristic that stood out to you in an odd way, or ones that have personal meaning to you. You can always look up the symbolism through your resources, too.
- Explain how your circles manifest themselves, making note of the particulars, as you set your intention for each circle, right up until you enter the mandorla.
- Describe the experience of being inside the mandorla, including comments on the energy, emotions, and feelings of being in that transformative space.
- What knowledge and insights are conveyed to you through this process? Are there personal realizations? A central message? A plan for how to proceed ahead?

◎ If you do the group variation, make a note of the two items you hold. Do not forget to write down the name of your partner for the meditation. Afterward, be sure to detail discoveries about your connection and any revealed synchronicity.

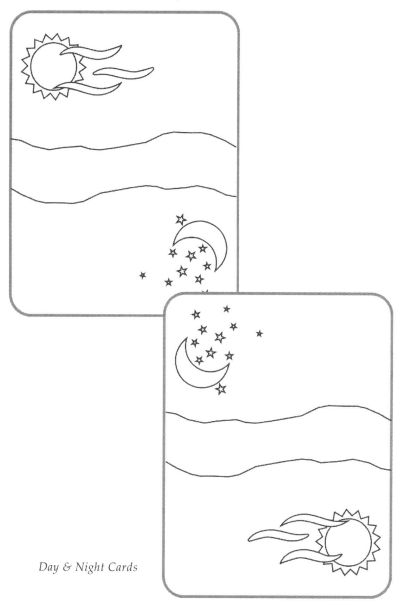

Day & Night Cards

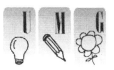

NIGHT to DAY MEDITATION

In unfamiliar darkness, we lean toward being cautious, anxious, or even frightened. When night breaks into day, what was concealed, obscured, or intimidating, transforms to what is recognizable. What we now identify becomes manageable and useful. In moments that we struggle, oftentimes a piece of the situation is yet unknown to us, rather like being in darkness. While we cannot force Divine timing, we can ask for guidance and make sure that we are open to insight and opportunity. So, think of this activity meditation as a means to shed light on an issue or challenge.

Using one of the Day & Night Card free online printables, like the ones shown on the previous page, write your questions or a topic for meditation on the nighttime half of the image. This represents what is hidden or unknown to you as of yet. (See page 266 for printables information).

Your meditation begins in a nighttime setting. If you wish to start with an absolute void, you may. However, if you prefer meditating on this somewhere familiar—at least in the pitch-black darkness—you can certainly find your first door to the right in your *Hallway* (page 56) by touch alone. It may even be helpful or inspiring, to see your familiar path in the dark. This could potentially present a new perspective, guidance of a nocturnal totem animal, such as fireflies, bats, and red pandas. It may even bring about symbolic messages of constellations, shadow shapes, or any other number of possibilities for insights not generally visible in the daylight.

Over the course of the meditation, the lighting should gradually increase to some extent, if not ending in full light. Allow the progression of imagery to lead you where it will as clarity emerges regarding your question.

When you are ready to finish, shift your awareness back to your breathing and physical body. Feel that sense of lightness and connectedness once again before opening your eyes.

Write your insights on the "Day" side of the card and sketch in the symbols or scenery to finish your session.

For Your Journal

◎ Did you try your meditation beginning from the dark void or did you opt for going through your door in the hallway?
◎ If from the void—what were the first things you perceived—whether by sight, sound, or feel?
  o How did this journey for you progress from darkness to light?
  o What aspects and sensory findings helped you to gain information about your initial question?
◎ If you decided to go through the hallway to your personal space, describe all the new aspects you were able to perceive by being in the dark that you had not noticed during previous "well-lit" meditation. What is accessible or visible in the nighttime setting that was not so noticeable with the daylight?

- o At what stages or points of your walk does light or visibility increase? Is there a correlation between that and noticing symbolic features or acquiring information along the way?
- Upon the start of your meditation, which of your senses or ultra-senses were helping you navigate your way, or which ones were more keenly receptive? Were you aware of smells or tastes?
- How do feelings of doubt, hesitation, insecurity, or fear shift through the course of the meditation?
- Did you feel like anything was hindering your progression? If so, how did this evolve throughout the meditation? Do you find a parallel to this with your present circumstance or concern?
- What is the most important bit of information brought to light and how are you able to use this regarding your starting topic?
- Be sure to use an affirmation if it will help you in the coming days until your issue or challenge is resolved.

DAY to NIGHT MEDITATION

While the Night to Day Meditation brings light to an issue in life, the Day to Night Meditation allows us to move past the conscious, analytical, and visible, to a place or perspective of greater stillness, peace, openness, and magic. It is perfect for purposes of healing and awakening our spirit.

Again, you will use a Day & Night card printable (like the examples shown on page 251). This time, on the daytime side of the card, write your question regarding your health or spirituality, for which you would like help and guidance.

Once you are all set to begin your meditation, concentrate on an ancient outdoor observatory or great stone circle coming into focus as your surroundings. It being fully daylight, you are welcome to walk around the area a bit, taking in whatever features or happenings are prominent to you. Gradually, day will lapse into night, so before it does become too dark you will want to come to rest at the center of the circle. There you can either sit or lie down in the grass to relax. As daylight gives way to night, maybe you will even see the Milky Way or Aurora Borealis. Depending on your topic—healing or spirituality—you may find yourself observing and participating, patient or student. Be open to the healing or growth process that is presented to you. Ask questions as needed.

When your session comes to a close, thank the healing guides or spirit mentors who have helped you. Returning from there should happen easily as you shift your consciousness forward.

With the "Night" side of your card, sketch symbols or scenery to complete your picture. In addition, record the advice or information revealed so you will have this to refer to as you continue your process of healing or spiritual growth in the days to follow.

For Your Journal

- Either attach your card into your journal or transfer the information onto a journal page.
- Describe your ancient observatory and the surrounding area you explored.
- Include your experience in the circle. Did you have guides or mentors that came to work with you? If so, be sure to include details, especially if it was someone new to you.
- Write a little about the shift from day to night—from the daylight aspect of the conscious to the nighttime aspect of the subconscious. What new perspectives of mystery, peace, and higher awareness do you experience?
- How do you feel your sensory or ultra-sensory perception shifts in parallel with this transition?
- Regarding meditations for healing purposes, look up additional information on colors that played a role in your meditation using the *Color Guide* (page 267). Color could also play a role in spiritual awakening, so if this is the case, extra insights about the color are often of value, too.

Part Four

Meditation Materials & Resources

INDEX of MEDITATIONS
Alphabetical

INDEX of MEDITATIONS
by Purpose & Need

MEDITATION RESOURCES

For your convenience, free printables designed to accompany certain activity meditations are available to you online at: www.MandorlaAcademy.com/shop.

Meditation	Page #	Printable
Day to Night	255	Day & Night Card
Doodle	74	More Doodles
Echo	94	Song Lyric Cut-Outs
Healing Heart	142	Healing Hearts
Labyrinth	111	Labyrinth (color)
Lyrical Meditation	170	Song Lyric Cut-Outs
More Than a Door	86	Door Cards (color)
Night to Day	252	Day & Night Card
What Others Need	199	Phrase Papers

APPENDIX

Use the guides in this appendix to help you interpret symbolism you encounter during your meditative experiences. As you read a certain listing, look to see which word or phrase instantly carries meaning for you. If you are uncertain, you can always throw the question out to the Universe to ask for a sign of the significance—usually you will have your answer within a day or two.

Color Guide: Idioms & Meanings

BLACK

Concentration, introspection, seriousness, mystery, the unknown, mourning, unconscious, malice, guilt, resentment

black-hearted	: wicked
in the black	: out of financial danger
black sheep	: outcast

BLUE

Communication, harmony, patience, devotion, sincerity, truth, devotion, tranquility, openness, clarity

out of the blue	: with no warning
blue skies	: happiness
singing the blues	: sadness, melancholy

BROWN

Earthiness, obstinacy, practicality, worldliness, conservatism

in a brown study	: contemplation
brown-nose	: flatterer
brown-bag it	: brought from home

GRAY

Fear, fright, depression, ambivalence, detachment

gray area	: murky or undefined
get gray hair	: stressed-out
gray matter	: intellect

GREEN

Nature, renewal, regeneration, balance, sympathy, luck, prosperity, growth, health, healing, hope, vigor, serenity

to be green	: novice, immature
green thumb	: adept at growing plants
green light	: safe to proceed

ORANGE

Fertility, hope, new beginnings, vitality, attraction, friendliness, courtesy, liveliness, sociability, energy

PINK, ROSE

Love, joy, sweetness, affection, gentleness, happiness, compassion, romance, infatuation

tickled pink	: pleased, delighted
in the pink	: good health
rose-colored glasses	: optimism

PURPLE

Authority, mysticism, sentimentality, responsibility, nostalgia, devotion, loving, kindness, compassion, dignity

purple heart	: bravery
purple passion	: extravagant
purple prose	: embellished, flowery

<u>RED</u>

Vitality, passion, anger, sex, ecstasy, sensuality, activity, work, strength, courage, force, vigor, aggression, power

red carpet	: royal treatment
to be in the red	: financial trouble, overextended
red flag	: danger

<u>WHITE</u>

Purity, faith, enlightenment, perfection, innocence, peace, cleanliness, awareness

white lie	: harmless
lily white	: innocent, pure
white elephant	: useless

<u>YELLOW</u>

Intellect, joy, optimism, harmony, wisdom, agility, clarity, understanding

to be yellow	: sensational, melodramatic
yellow streak	: cowardly
yellow dog	: jealous, cowardly

Quick-Check Animal Symbolism Guide

This is an abbreviated list of symbolism keywords relevant to certain animals and animal spirits. As you read the listed words pertaining to an animal, see which one stands out to you in the moment. Not all of them will apply in any one given circumstance. The list is incomplete, so if you do not find an animal you are searching for, or if you would like more information about a certain animal, see the Great Resources section for additional references.

All animals, including those that are extinct or mythological, potentially bring personal and spiritual meaning to us through their symbolism. When they appear in our lives, they bring messages to us to let us know what they are trying to help us notice, learn, exemplify, or exude. The bear, cat, swan, and meadowlark especially guide and encourage us to meditate and to find answers within. Along with the swan, several animals are of unique significance when it comes to ultra-sensory development, including the cat, elephant, owl, snake, turtle, and catfish. Perhaps you have already noticed one of them guiding you along your journey.

⊙ A-B-C ⊙

Ant: diligence, patience, planning, routine
Bear: instinct, introspection, leadership, motherhood
Bee: concentration, interconnection, prosperity, rebirth
Bison, Buffalo: abundance, courage, generosity, survival
Bluejay: messages of guidance, spiritual growth, use caution
Butterfly: hopefulness, joy, reincarnation, transformation
Cat: clairvoyance, a healing nature, independence, love

⊙ D-E ⊙

Deer: grace, gratitude and giving, innocence, softness
Dog: companionship, friendship, love, loyalty
Dolphin: balance, harmony, optimism, spiritual guidance
Dragon: advocating, bravery, destiny, passion
Dragonfly: awareness, dream messages, new perspective
Duck: emotional clarity, fertility, stability, stillness
Eagle: aspirations, life purpose, positive transition, wisdom
Elephant: clairsentience, devotion, family bonds, strength

⊙ F-G-H ⊙

Fish: fertility, harmony, regeneration, love, variety
    Catfish (specifically): clairgustance
Fox: ingenuity, innocence, observation, originality
Frog: cleansing, sensitivity, steps to a goal, longevity
Grasshopper: following your passion, health, leap of faith
Gryphon: enlightenment, guardian, insight, soul-searching
Hawk: creativity, opportunity, spirit messages, vigilance
Horse: adventure and travel, endurance, passion, sociability

◎ L-M-O-P ◎

Lion: energy, pride, self-fulfillment, superiority
Monkey: charm, family bonds, playfulness, unity
Opossum: neutrality, recognizing gifts, recovery, viewpoint
Owl: attentiveness, claircognizance, renewal, self-esteem
Panther: beauty, clairaudience, grace, self-empowerment
Pegasus: astral travel, guidance, humility, inspiration
Phoenix: dignity, perseverance, progress, transformation

◎ R-S ◎

Rabbit: agility, creativity, improving ultra-senses, fertility
Raccoon: curiosity, dexterity, disguise, seeking guidance
Salamander: cooperation, perseverance, secrecy, subtlety
         Represents the element of fire, which has to do with
         primal energy, creativity, growth, endeavors and work
Sheep: kindness, sensitivity, new beginnings, productivity
Snake: clairolience, instinct, transition, self-reliance
Spider: agility, creativity, intricacy, knowledge
Squirrel: discovery, imagination, prudence, puzzle solving

◎ T-U-W ◎

Tiger: bravery, energy, power, leadership
Turtle: clairaudience, clairolience, clairvoyance, patience, life
Unicorn: artistic ability, dreams/dreaming, inner child, peace
Whale: assurance, creation, intuition, music for healing
Wolf: intellect, poise, regard for family/community, survival

Numerology Chart

An abbreviated numerological chart to help you decipher the symbolism of numbers you encounter or receive as messages in your meditations. Each entry has a header indicating the main principle of that number. A keyword list of pertinent nouns and adjectives follows. When you want to discern a message, skim through the keyword list for your number to find the one or two words that stand out at that moment. (A symbolic message is not the keyword list in its entirety).

Usually if you read the list in a state of calmness, being open to receiving the information, it will work quite easily. If you are uncertain that you have selected the right words, however, you can always ask your spirit guide or the universe to send you a sign of validation.

Any time that you have a larger number given to you as a symbolic message, add the individual numbers together until you reduce it to one of these master numbers (1-9, 11, or 22). For example, the year 2020 is a 4, $160.35 is a 6, and September 9, 2011 is a 22.

○1○
To BEGIN

achievement, ambition, assertiveness, attaining, beginnings, center, confidence, courage, ego, energy, independent, individuality, strength, initiative, launch, leader, leadership, original, originality, opportunity, pioneering, prime, self-sufficiency, start

○ 2 ○
To COLLABORATE

acquaint with, artistic, balance, charm, cooperation, diplomacy, diversity, duality, following, friend, friendship, gentleness, guidance, harmony, kindness, mediating, mentoring, partnering, partnership, peaceful, receptivity, sensitivity, supportiveness, symmetry, tact, understanding

○ 3 ○
To THINK

action, adaptability, amiable, articulate, body/mind/spirit, completion, creative, energy, expression, growth, humor, imagination, inner strength, *joie de vivre*, life, optimism, self-exploration, sensitivity, social, triad, uplifting, vision, vitality, wholeness

○ 4 ○
To PLAN

ambition, application, building, constructive, decisive, determination, diligence, earthly, focus, founder, foundation, hard work, harmony, logical, methodical, order, organized, patient, practical, quartet, realistic, reliability, serious, service, settled, stability, steady, stoic, traditional

○ 5 ○
To PIONEER

activity, adventure, change, clever, daring, enthusiasm, entrepreneurship, expansion, experimental, freedom, impatient, influential, inquisitive, lively, new growth, progress, promoter, mankind, motivation, persuasiveness, progress, spontaneity, travel, unconventional, versatile

○ 6 ○
To EDUCATE

accepting, balanced, careful, caring, coaching, community, compromise, conventional, family, forgiving, group co-operation, happy, home, influence, love, marriage, nurturing, patient, protective, reliable, responsibility, service, successful, sympathy, tranquility

○ 7 ○
To EXAMINE

analysis, awareness, eccentricity, imaginative, insightful, inventive, knowledge, loner, mystical, observant, opportunity, philosophical, receptive, research, risk, scholarly, silence, solitude, specialist, spiritual depth, studious, thoughtful, understanding, unique, quirky

○ 8 ○
To RESOLVE

abundance, achievement, capability, confidence, control, decisive, determination, demanding, explanation, formal, initiate, judgmental, materialism, organizer, power, practical endeavors, professional, sharing, solution, status, stern, strength, stubbornness, wealth, worker

◦ 9 ◦
To UNDERSTAND

altruistic, artistic, benevolent, compassionate, completion, creative expression, duty, empathy, enduring, eternity, healing, humanitarian, inspiration, integrity, intuitive, multifaceted, productive, rational, resilient, role model, philanthropic, selfless, success, tenacity, understanding, universal, wisdom

◦ 11 ◦
To INSPIRE

achievement, advocate, awareness, dramatic, dreamer, emotional, energetic, enlightenment, healing, idealism, inspirational, intuitive, illumination, insight, optimism, perspective, poetic, radical, revelation, romantic, spirituality, transformation, truth, understanding

◦ 22 ◦
To EXEMPLIFY

accomplishment, aspiration, authority with grace, direction, discerning, endeavors, expansive, experienced, global thinking, guiding, influential, intent, leadership, maturity, perceptive, practical, purposeful, sophisticated, steady, unbiased, unconventional, vision, wise, worldly

Symbolism of Flowers & Trees

As a whole, **TREES** are long symbolic of life, strength, wisdom and growth. **FLOWERS** are representative of beauty, pleasure, giving, love, and appreciation. A nice, varied bouquet carries the meaning of good manners and respect; often given as a gesture of congratulations, or caring. The special thing about plants is that nearly all our senses might be used to experience them…or some might say *all*, depending on how closely you listen.

FLOWERS

○ A-B-C ○

Aster: diversity, patience
Begonia: reflection, ultra-sensory perception
Bluebell: forthcoming news, kindness
Buttercup: cheerfulness, childhood
Carnation: health
    Pink: motherhood
    Red: an affirmation
    White: charm
    Yellow: disdain
    Striped: indecision
Chrysanthemum: longevity
    Spider: wild abandon
    Red: love
    White: truth
    Yellow: unrequited love
Clematis: intellectual beauty

Columbine: playfulness

Cornflower (Bachelor's Button): delicacy

Crocus: hope

○ D-E-F ○

Daffodil: clarity

Dahlia: higher spiritual development

Daisy: inner strength

Dandelion: faithfulness

Fern: confidence

Forget-me-not: friendship

Foxglove: a wish

○ G-H-I ○

Gardenia: emotional guidance

Geranium: an unexpected encounter

Gladiola: willingness

Heather: healing from within, insight

Hibiscus: warmth

Honeysuckle: learning from the past

Hyacinth: overcoming grief

Hydrangea: boastfulness

Iris: a message

○ J-K-L ○

Jasmine: attachment, sensuality,

Kangaroo Paw: gentleness, originality

Larkspur: levity

Lavender: healing

Lilac: spirituality

Lily: peace

Lily-of-the-Valley: happiness

◎ M-N-O ◎

Marigold: creativity, grief

Morning Glory: spontaneity

Nasturtium: patriotism

Orchid: luxury, beauty

◎ P-Q-R ◎

Pansy: reflecting on a relationship

Peony: devotion

Primrose: youth

Rose: love

    White: admiration

    Yellow: friendship, joy

    Red: passion

    Pink: grace, new romance

    Mix of Varieties: gratitude, unity

◎ S-T-U ◎

Snapdragon: clairaudience, forgiveness

Snowdrop: purity

Sunflower: opportunity

Tulip: benevolence, affirmation

◎ V-W-X-Y-Z ◎

Vervain: charisma

Violet: fulfillment

Zinnia: nostalgia, remembrance

TREES

○ A-B-C ○

Acacia: clairsentience, empathy, secret love

Almond: Divine grace, hidden truth, the unknown

Apple: clairgustance, magnificence, temptation

Ash: higher wisdom, objectivity, sacrifice

Aspen: determination, overcoming obstacles, support

Beech: endurance, past knowledge, stability

Birch: gracefulness, new beginnings, soul-searching

Bottle Brush: abundance, humor, major life transition

Cedar: clairolience, cleansing, healing, protection

Cherry: education, reincarnation, spirituality

Cypress: overcoming grief, mourning, sacrifice

○ D-E-F ○

Elm: dignity, intuition, willpower

Elder: cycle of life, journey, progress, spiritual guidance

Eucalyptus: transformation, dilemma, dream messages

Fig: prosperity, reward, fulfilling dreams and desires

Fir: elevation, flexibility, clarity, clairaudience

○ G-H-I ○

Hawthorne: defense, fertility, magic

Hazel: creativity, compromise, dowsing and divination

Holly: overcoming anger, premonition, spiritual warrior

○ J-K-L ○

Laurel: accomplishment, perseverance, victory

Linden: faithfulness, friendship, watched over

◎ M-N-O ◎

Maple: balance, practical higher awareness
Oak: bravery, claircognizance, Divine presence, strength
Olive: honesty, justice, peace, well-being
Orange: emotional clarity, generosity, sweetness

◎ P-Q-R ◎

Palm: opportunity, peace, protection, victory
Pine: creativity, morality, perspective
Plum: eagerness, good luck, happiness
Poplar: courage, faith, time
Redwood: ancient wisdom, longevity

◎ S-T-U ◎

Spruce: healing, new awareness, ultra-sensory insight
Sycamore: communication, curiosity, learning to receive
Tamarack: awakening, hope, rebirth

◎ V-W-X-Y-Z ◎

Walnut: intellect, welcoming change, your own path
Willow: clairvoyance, healing, imagination
Water Willow: freedom, melancholy, openness
Yew: eternal life, resolving past issues, sadness

◎ Also ◎

Acorn: growing strength or courage, immortality, life
Cactus: manifesting prosperity, protection, survival
Fern: magic, self-confidence, shelter, sincerity, surprise
Ivy: affection, faithfulness, friendship, inner strength
Seeds: beginning, hope, promise, potential, waiting

GREAT RESOURCES

Build your library of resources to help you discover hidden meanings and symbolism within your meditations. These are a few great options online and in print to start:

WEBSITES:
Animal Spirits
   www.animalspirits.com
Symbols.com
   www.symbols.com
DreamMoods Dream Dictionary
   www.dreammoods.com/dreamdictionary
Ravenari's Animal Guide
   www.wildspeak.com/animaldictionary.html

BOOKS:
Dream Dictionary: An A to Z Guide to Understanding Your Unconscious Mind by Tony Crisp

Linda Goodman's Love Signs: A New Approach to the Human Heart by Linda Goodman.

Pocket Guide to Spirit Animals: Understanding Messages from Your Animal Spirit Guides by Dr. Steven Farmer.

Totem Animal Messages: Channeled Messages from the Animal Kingdom by Brigit Goldworthy.

GLOSSARY of TERMS

Archangel: An angel of elevated distinction having specialized interests or capability in helping humanity; overseer of other angels who watch over us.

Ascended master: A person who lived a life as a healer, spiritual teacher, or prophet, and is now in spirit continuing to guide humanity.

Bibliomancy: Divination by opening a book to a random page and reading a passage. The prefix *biblio-* specifically refers to using a bible for this purpose.

Chakra: The energy centers of the body (aura) through which life energy flows in and out.

Clairaudience: The ability to distinguish sound by ultra-sensory means; the faculty of hearing something not perceptible to the ear; "clear-hearing."
From French, *clair* (clear) + Latin, *audire* (to hear)

Claircognizance: The ultra-sense of knowing; the sixth sense; "clear-knowing."
From French, *clair* (clear) + Latin, *cognoscere* (to know)

Clairgustance: The ability to taste by ultra-sensory means; "clear-tasting."
From French, *clair* (clear) + Latin, *gustare* (to taste)

Clairolience: The ability to smell by ultra-sensory means; "clear-smelling."

From French, *clair* (clear) + Latin, *olere* (to smell)

Clairsentience: The ability to perceive physical and emotional feelings by ultra-sensory means; "clear-feeling." From French, clair (clear) + Latin, *sentire* (to feel)

Clairvoyance: The ability to see by ultra-sensory means; seeing through the "mind's eye"; "clear-seeing." From French, *clair* (clear) + Latin, *videre* (to see)

Divination: The practice of acquiring information about past, present, or future, by ultra-sensory means and/or by using tools of divination, such as tarot cards or runes.

Higher self (the Self): A person's soul, the Divine or complete spirit; one's spiritual whole; differentiated from the Earthly human personality and ordinary essence of being.

Infused Thought: Telepathic communication allowing those in spirit to send a human being words, ideas, or imagery.

Oneness: The interconnectedness of all living beings, the connection existing between all life in the Universe.

Precognition: Perception of future events by ultra-sensory means; generally occurring unintentionally.

Premonition: Synonymous with precognition, although forewarning is often implied.

Remote Viewing (Natural or Psychic): The ability to access or gather information about events, scenes, people, places, etc., using ultra-sensory means over a distance of time and/or space.

Soul Agreement: The arrangement made between two souls before entering a human lifetime, with intention of helping to fulfill life purposes. These can be simple or complex.

Synchronicity: Divine timing; a sequence of related and meaningful, remarkable or unexpected events.

Telepathy: Non-verbal communication between a sender and receiver; communicating by using ultra-sensory means to transfer emotional, mental, or physical messages.

Ultra-Senses: Senses perceived beyond the range or limits of ordinary or moderate physical sensory perception; sensory experience at a higher frequency than common human experience.

Universal Mind: A shared collective consciousness of which we are all a part; where knowledge resides; access or attunement enables knowledge beyond our physical, conventional means.

BIBLIOGRAPHY

Andrews, Ted. *Animal Speak: The Spiritual and Magical Powers of Creatures Great & Small.* St. Paul: Llewellyn Publications, 1996.

Artress, Rev. Dr. Lauren, and John Rhodes. World-Wide Labyrinth Locator. www.labyrinthlocator.com.

Chan, Amanda. "Mindfulness Meditation Benefits: 20 Reasons Why It's Good for Your Mental and Physical Health." *Huffington Post.* (8 April 2013). http://www.huffingtonpost.com/2013/04/08/mindfulness-meditation-benefits-health_n_3016045.html

Dean, Liz. *The Mystery of the Tarot.* New York: Barnes & Noble Books, 2003.

DeSteno, David. "The Morality of Meditation." *NYTimes.com.* (5 July 2013). http://www.nytimes.com/2013/07/07/opinion/sunday/the-morality-of-meditation.html?_r=0

Goldworthy, Brigit. *Totem Animal Messages: Channeled Messages from the Animal Kingdom.* Bloomington, IN: Balboa Press, 2013.

Goodman, Linda. *Linda Goodman's Love Signs: A New Approach to the Human Heart.* New York, NY: HarperPerennial, 1992.

Illes, Judika. *Encyclopedia of Spirits: The Ultimate Guide to the Magic of Fairies, Genies, Demons, Ghosts, Gods & Goddesses.* New York: Harper One, 2009.

Johnson, Robert A. *Owning Your Own Shadow: Understanding the Dark Side of the Psyche.* San Francisco: Harper, 1991.

King, Francis X. *The Encyclopedia of Fortune Telling.* New York: Gallery Books, 1988.

The Language of Flowers. http://aggie-horticulture.tamu.edu/archives/parsons/publications/flowers/flowers.html

The Language of Flowers. http://www.languageofflowers.com/flower meaning.htm#anchora

Liungman, Carl G. *Dictionary of Symbols.* New York: W.W. Norton & Company, 1991.

McClain, Michael. Astrology-Numerology. www.astrology-numerology.com

Millman, Dan. *The Life You Were Born to Live: A Guide to the Thirty-Seven Pathways of Life and How to Find Yours.* New York: MJF Books, 1993.

Moorey, Teresa. *The Numerology Bible: The Definitive Guide to the Power of Numbers.* New York: Firefly Books, 2012.

Numerology Guide. www.numerology-guide.com/numerology_number_meanings.htm

Peschek-Böhmer, Dr. Flora and Gisela Schreiber. *Healing Crystals and Gemstones from Amethyst to Zircon.* Old Saybrook, CT : Konecky & Konecky, 2003.

Powell, Claire. *The Meaning of Flowers: A Garland of Plant Lore & Symbolism from Popular Custom & Literature.* Boulder, CO: Shambhala, 1979.

AN AFTERWORD

As you may have already guessed, my personal door in *The Hallway* is blue—a dark, distressed, cobalt blue color with lovely medieval metalwork. After more than seventeen years of writing, channeling, and collecting these meditations and many more, I find myself continually guided to write new ones still. It appears there is a limitless amount of possibility for our meditative journeys; it should come as no surprise in this infinite world in which we live. I am happy you have found yourself winding through this inclusive and remarkable circle of kindred spirits and hope you will enjoy using the meditations in *Through the Blue Door* for many years to come.

My warmest appreciation to my spirit guides who, very generously and patiently, continue to teach me and have conveyed these meditations, so that I might share them.

Deepest gratitude…to those students and clients who graciously responded to my request for their meditation experiences, sharing their personal stories so that we all grow and learn more. Your words will bring light to others,

…to my Light Source students who journeyed through these meditations together every week over so many years, giving rise to all the possibilities for meditation,

…to my dear friends, Donelle and Claudia, who were the voice of encouragement through the lulls, frustrations, and milestones of writing; and to my sister for fielding random technical and design questions,

…to Kristin and Adrianne and their wonderful staff at County Seat Coffeehouse, who keep me fully caffeinated,

…to my person, for bringing me hope and love across lifetimes, and inspiring me to see this through,

…and especially to my son, who was ever such a good sport and more patient than any child should have to be, while I was busy teaching the classes that were the foundation for these meditations. There will always be a gift waiting in your tree. Thank you for making everything worthwhile.

Beyond this, I humbly invite you to visit my website, MandorlaAcademy.com. In the shop, you will find the free printables, as well as the *Through the Blue Door Companion Journal*, which will supply you with pages for recording your meditations, and 58 more journaling prompts.

Once you navigate some of the meditations in *Through the Blue Door*, please submit your own meditation stories there, like those found in this book. Select stories will be featured in upcoming books in the series. The submission form and ideas for what to write about are on the "Meditations Stories" page under the *Blue Door Blog*.

Additional articles, including 20-Minute Meditation Playlists with ideas for complementary, guided meditations, and a depth of articles are also found there. They cover a wide range of metaphysical and spiritual topics.

In closing, were we in a workshop, I would recommend trying those opening four steps periodically. You will see how much your ability grows over time; it is a great way to validate all your hard work.

I wish you many happy meditative adventures and a peace-filled life!

Heather

www.MandorlaAcademy.com
Facebook: www.facebook.com/minnesotamedium

ABOUT the AUTHOR

Heather Oelschlager is a professional psychic medium and spiritual consultant who lives in southern Minnesota. She specializes in non-traditional grief support and life concerns, working with clients worldwide. Ultra-sensory meditations are woven throughout her classes on grief and loss, past lives, dream interpretation, spiritual and psychic development, and many other metaphysical topics.

At Bemidji State University, Heather studied languages, going on to work in the travel industry and education, before making the move to consulting full-time. She enjoys walking a good labyrinth, taking road trips and attending concerts with her son, and chatting with friends over coffee. Heather has also been known to take a few photos and make a bit of art.

"How infinitely superior to our physical sense are those of the mind."
- John Muir

ART PRINTS

Full-color art prints of select illustrations from the *Blue Door* meditation book series are available for purchase. Visit MandorlaAcademy.com for information.

Made in the USA
Middletown, DE
24 July 2023

35646037R00163